PEN
The Perpetua
C000254104

Jorge Luis Borges

1899–1986

Jorge Luis Borges

The Perpetual Race of Achilles and the Tortoise

TRANSLATED BY ESTHER ALLEN, SUZANNE JILL LEVINE
AND ELIOT WEINBERGER

PENGUIN BOOKS — GREAT IDEAS

PENGUIN BOOKS

Published by the Penguin Group
Penguin Books Ltd, 80 Strand, London WC2R ORL, England
Penguin Group (USA) Inc., 375 Hudson Street, New York, New York 10014, USA
Penguin Group (Canada), 90 Eglinton Avenue East, Suite 700, Toronto, Ontario, Canada M4P 2Y3
(a division of Pearson Penguin Canada Inc.)
Penguin Ireland, 25 St Stephen's Green, Dublin 2, Ireland (a division of Penguin Books Ltd)
Penguin Group (Australia), 250 Camberwell Road, Camberwell, Victoria 3124,
Australia (a division of Pearson Australia Group Pty Ltd)
Penguin Books India Pvt Ltd, 11 Community Centre,
Panchsheel Park, New Delhi – 110 017, India
Penguin Group (NZ), 67 Apollo Drive, Rosedale, North Shore 0632, New Zealand
(a division of Pearson New Zealand Ltd)
Penguin Books (South Africa) (Pty) Ltd, 24 Sturdee Avenue, Rosebank, Johannesburg 2196, South Africa

Penguin Books Ltd, Registered Offices: 30 Strand, London WC2R ORL, England

www.penguin.com

Taken from *The Total Library: Non-Fiction 1922–1986* first published
by Allen Lane 1999
This selection published in Penguin Books 2010

002

'The Translators of *The Thousand and One Nights*', 'Our Poor Individualism', 'On Oscar
Wilde' and 'The Enigma of Shakespeare' translated by Esther Allen

'The Perpetual Race of Achilles and the Tortoise', 'Two Films', 'A Pedagogy of Hatred', 'A
Comment on August 23, 1944' and 'An Overwhelming Film' translated by Suzanne Jill Levine

'The Duration of Hell' translated by Suzanne Jill Levine and Eliot Weinberger

'A Defense of Basilides the False', 'The Labyrinths of the Detective Story and
Chesterton', 'Joyce's Latest Novel', 'On William Beckford's *Vathek*', 'The Wall and the
Books', 'The Innocence of Layamon', 'Coleridge's Dream' and 'Blindness' translated by
Eliot Weinberger

English translations copyright © Esther Allen, Suzanne Jill Levine, Eliot Weinberger, 1999

Set in 11/13 Dante MT Std
Typeset by TexTech International
Printed in England by Clays Ltd, St Ives plc

ISBN: 978-0-141-19294-9

www.greenpenguin.co.uk

MIX
Paper from
responsible sources
FSC™ C018179
www.fsc.org

Penguin Books is committed to a sustainable
future for our business, our readers and our planet.
This book is made from Forest Stewardship
Council™ certified paper.

ALWAYS LEARNING   **PEARSON**

Contents

1. The Perpetual Race of Achilles and the Tortoise   1
2. The Duration of Hell   9
3. A Defense of Basilides the False   15
4. The Translators of *The Thousand and One Nights*   21
5. The Labyrinths of the Detective Story and Chesterton   50
6. Two Films (*Crime and Punishment* and *The Thirty-Nine Steps*)   55
7. Joyce's Latest Novel   57
8. A Pedagogy of Hatred   59
9. A Comment on August 23, 1944   61
10. On William Beckford's *Vathek*   64
11. An Overwhelming Film (*Citizen Kane*)   69
12. Our Poor Individualism   71
13. On Oscar Wilde   74
14. The Wall and the Books   78
15. The Innocence of Layamon   82

Contents

16. Coleridge's Dream   88
17. The Enigma of Shakespeare   94
18. Blindness   111

The Perpetual Race of Achilles
and the Tortoise

The implications of the word *jewel* – precious little thing, delicate though not necessarily fragile, easy to transport, translucency that can also be impenetrable, ageless flower – make it pertinent here. I know of no better qualification for Achilles' paradox, so indifferent to the definitive refutations which have been nullifying it for over twenty-three centuries that we can already declare it immortal. The repeated tours of the mystery proposed by such endurance, the fine ignorance it has visited upon humanity, are gifts we have no choice but to accept gratefully. Let us revive it once more, if only to convince ourselves of perplexity and arcane intimations. I intend to devote a few pages – a few moments – to its presentation and most noteworthy revisions. Its inventor, as is well known, was Zeno of Elea, disciple of Parmenides, who denied that anything could happen in the universe.

The library has provided me with two versions of this glorious paradox. The first, from a very Spanish Spanish-American dictionary, can be reduced to this cautious observation: *Motion does not exist: Achilles could not catch up with the lazy tortoise.* I shall waive such restraint and seek out the less hurried exposition by G. H. Lewes, whose *Biographical History of Philosophy* was the first speculative reading to which vanity or curiosity (I'm not sure which) led me. I shall transcribe his exposition: Achilles, symbol of speed, has to catch up with the tortoise, symbol of slowness. Achilles runs ten times faster than the tortoise and so gives him a ten-meter advantage. Achilles runs those ten meters, the tortoise runs one; Achilles runs that meter, the tortoise runs a decimeter; Achilles runs that decimeter, the tortoise runs a centimeter; Achilles runs that centimeter, the tortoise runs a millimeter; Achilles the millimeter, the tortoise a tenth of the millimeter and *ad infinitum*, so that Achilles can run forever without catching up. Hence the immortal paradox.

And now for the so-called refutations. The oldest – Aristotle's and Hobbes' – are implicit in the one formulated by John Stuart Mill. The problem, for him, is a mere example of the fallacy of confusion. He considers it nullified by the following argument:

At the conclusion of the sophism, *forever* means any imaginable lapse of time; under this premise, any number of subdivisions of time. It means that we can divide ten units by ten, and the quotient again by ten, as many times as we want, and that the subdivisions of the sequence have no end, nor consequently do those of the time in which it all occurs. But an unlimited number of subdivisions can occur within what is limited. The only infinity of duration the argument proves is contained in five minutes. As long as the five minutes are not over, whatever is left can be divided by ten, and again by ten, as many times as we like, which is compatible with the fact that the total duration is five minutes. This proves, in short, that crossing that finite space requires an infinitely divisible, but not infinite, time (Mill, *System of Logic* V, chap. 7).

I cannot predict the reader's opinion, but my feeling is

that Mill's projected refutation is nothing more than an exposition of the paradox. Achilles' speed need only be set at a second per meter to determine the time needed:

$$10 + 1 + 1/10 + 1/100 + 1/1000 + 1/10000 \ldots$$

The limit of the sum of this infinite geometric progression is twelve (plus, exactly eleven and one-fifth; plus, exactly eleven times three twenty-fifths), but it is never reached. That is, the hero's course will be infinite and he will run forever, but he will give up before twelve meters, and his eternity will not see the end of twelve seconds. That methodical dissolution, that boundless descent into more and more minute precipices, is not really hostile to the problem; imagining it is the problem. Let us not forget, either, to visualize the runners diminishing, not only because of perspective but also because of the singular reduction required by their occupation of microscopic places. Let us also realize that those linked precipices corrupt space and, even more vertiginously, living time, in their desperate persecution of both immobility and ecstasy.

Another resolute refutation was divulged in 1910 by Henri Bergson, in his noteworthy *Essay on the Immediate Facts of Consciousness*, a title that begins by begging the question. Here is his page:

On the one hand, we attribute to motion the very divisibility of the space it traverses, forgetting that while an object can be divided, an action cannot. On the other hand, we are accustomed to projecting this very action upon space, applying it to the line traversed by the moving object, to giving it, in brief, solid form. Out of this confusion between motion and the space traversed are born, in our opinion, the sophisms of the Eleatic School: because the interval separating two points is infinitely divisible, and if motion were composed of parts as the interval is, the interval would never be traversed. But the truth is that each of Achilles' steps is a simple indivisible action, and that after a given number of these actions, Achilles would have gotten ahead of the tortoise. The Eleatic illusion came from identifying this series of individual actions *sui generis* with the homogeneous space that served as their stage. As such a space can be divided and reconstituted according to any law, they assumed the authority to redo Achilles' total movement, no longer with Achilles' steps but with tortoise steps. They replaced Achilles in pursuit of a tortoise with two tortoises at regular intervals from one another, two tortoises agreeing to make the same kind of steps or simultaneous actions so as never to catch up with each other. Why does Achilles get ahead of the tortoise? Because each of Achilles' steps and each of the tortoise's steps are indivisible as movements, and different magnitudes in space: so that it will not take long for the sum of space traversed by Achilles to be a superior length to the sum of space traversed by the tortoise and of the advantage the latter had over him. Which is what Zeno does not have in mind when reconstructing Achilles' motion according to the same law as the tortoise's motion, forgetting that only space lends itself to a mode of arbitrary construction and deconstruction, confusing it thus with motion. (*Immediate Facts*, Barnes' Spanish version, pp. 89–90. I've corrected, by the way, some obvious lapses by the translator.)

Bergson's argument is a compromise. He admits that space is infinitely divisible, but denies that time is. He displays two tortoises instead of one to distract the reader. He links a time and a space that are incompatible: the abrupt discontinuous time of William James, with its 'perfect effervescence of newness,' and the infinitely divisible space in common credence.

Here I reach, by elimination, the only refutation I know, the only inspiration worthy of the original, a virtue indispensable for the aesthetics of intelligence: the one formulated by Bertrand Russell. I found it in the noble work of William James (*Some Problems of Philosophy*) and the total conception it postulates can be studied in the previous books of its inventor – *Introduction to Mathematical Philosophy*, 1919; *Our Knowledge of the External World*, 1926 – unsatisfactory, intense books, inhumanly lucid. For Russell, the operation of counting is (intrinsically) that of equating two series. For example, if the first-born sons of all the houses of Egypt were killed by the Angel, except those who lived in a house that had a red mark on the door, it is clear that as many sons were saved as there were red marks, and an enumeration of precisely how many of these there were does not matter. Here the quantity is indefinite; there are other operations in which it is infinite as well. The natural series of numbers is infinite, but we can demonstrate that, within it, there are as many odd numbers as even ones.

1	corresponds to	2
3	to	4
5	to	6, etc.

The proof is as irreproachable as it is banal, but does not differ from the following, in which there are as many multiples of 3018 as there are numbers.

1	corresponds to	3018
2	to	6036
3	to	9054
4	to	12072, etc.

The same can be asserted about its exponential powers, however rarified they become as we progress.

1	corresponds to	3018
2	to	3018^2 (9,108,324)
3	to	etc.

A jocose acceptance of these facts has inspired the formula that an infinite collection – that is, the series of natural numbers – is a collection whose members can in turn be broken down into infinite series. The part, in these elevated latitudes of numeration, is no less copious than the whole: the precise quantity of points in the universe is the same as in a meter in the universe, or in a decimeter, or in the deepest trajectory of a star. Achilles' problem fits within this heroic response. Each place occupied by the tortoise is in proportion to another occupied by Achilles, and the meticulous correspondence of both symmetrical series, point by point, serves to proclaim their equality. There does not remain one single periodic remnant of the initial advantage given to the tortoise. The final point in his course, the last in Achilles' course and the last in the time of the race, are terms which coincide mathematically: this is Russell's solution. James, without negating the technical superiority of *his* opponent, chooses to disagree. Russell's statements (he writes) elude the real difficulty concerning the *growing*, not the *stable*, category of infinity, the only one he takes into consideration when presuming that the race has been run and that the problem is to equilibrate the courses. On the other hand, two are not needed: the course of each runner or the mere lapse of empty time implies the difficulty of reaching a goal when a previous interval continues presenting itself at every turn, obstructing the way (*Some Problems of Philosophy* [1911], 181).

I have reached the end of my article, but not of our speculation. The paradox of Zeno of Elea, as James indicated, is an attempt upon not only the reality of space but the more invulnerable and sheer reality of time. I might add that existence in a physical body, immobile permanence, the flow of an afternoon in life, are challenged by such an adventure. Such a deconstruction, by means of only one word, *infinite*, a worrisome word (and then a concept) we have engendered fearlessly, once it besets our thinking, explodes and annihilates it. (There are other ancient punishments against commerce with such a treacherous word: there is the Chinese legend of the scepter of the kings of Liang, reduced to half its size by each new king. The scepter, mutilated by dynasties, still prevails.) My opinion, after the supremely qualified ones I have presented, runs the double risk of appearing impertinent and trivial. I will nonetheless formulate it: Zeno is incontestable, unless we admit the ideality of space and time. If we accept idealism, if we accept the concrete growth of the perceived, then we shall elude the *mise en abîme* of the paradox.

Would this bit of Greek obscurity affect our concept of the universe? – my reader will ask.

[1929]

The Duration of Hell

Hell has become, over the years, a wearisome speculation. Even its proselytizers have neglected it, abandoning the poor, but serviceable, human allusion which the ecclesiastic fires of the Holy Office once had in this world: a temporal torment, of course, but one that was not unworthy, within its terrestrial limitations, of being a metaphor for the immortal, for the perfect pain without destruction that the objects of divine wrath will forever endure. Whether or not this hypothesis is satisfactory, an increasing lassitude in the propaganda of the institution is indisputable. (Do not be alarmed; I use *propaganda* here not in its commercial but rather its Catholic genealogy: a congregation of cardinals.) In the second century A.D., the Carthaginian Tertullian could imagine Hell and its proceedings with these words:

> You who are fond of spectacles, expect the greatest of all spectacles, the last and eternal judgment of the universe. How shall I admire, how laugh, how rejoice, how exult, when I behold so many proud monarchs, and fancied gods, groaning in the lowest abyss of darkness; so many magistrates who persecuted the name of the Lord, liquefying in fiercer fires than they ever kindled against the Christians; so many sage philosophers blushing in red hot flames with their deluded scholars; so many celebrated

9

poets trembling before the tribunal, not of Minos, but of
Christ; so many tragedians, more tuneful in the expression of their own sufferings; so many dancers . . . (*De
spectaculis*, 30; Gibbon's version.)

Dante himself, in his great effort to foresee, in an anecdo-
tal way, some of the decisions of Divine Justice regarding
northern Italy, did not know such enthusiasm. Later, the literary infernos of Quevedo – a mere opportunity for gossipy
anachronisms – and of Torres Villarroel – a mere opportunity for metaphors – would only prove the increasing usury
of dogma. The decline of Hell is in their works, as it is in
Baudelaire, who was so skeptical about the perpetual tor-
ments that he pretended to adore them. (In a significant ety-
mology, the innocuous French verb *gêner* [to bother] derives
from that powerful Scriptural word, *Gehenna*.)

Let us consider Hell. The careless article on the subject in the *Hispano-American Encyclopedic Dictionary* is useful reading, not for its sparse information or terrified
sacristan's theology but rather for the bewilderment it
discloses. It begins by observing that the notion of Hell
is not particular to the Catholic Church, a precaution
whose intrinsic meaning is, *Don't let the Masons say the
Church introduced these atrocities*; but this is immediately
followed by the statement that Hell is dogma, and it
quickly adds: 'The unwithering glory of Christianity is
that it brings to itself all the truths to be found scattered
among the false religions.' Whether Hell is a fact of natural religion, or only of revealed religion, I find no other
theological assumption as fascinating or as powerful. I
am not referring to the simplistic mythology of manure,

roasting spits, fires, and tongs, which have gone on prolif-
erating in the depths, and which all writers have repeated,
to the dishonor of their imaginations and their decency.[1]
I am speaking of the strict notion – *a place of eternal
punishment for the wicked* – constituted by the dogma with
no other obligation than placing it *in loco real*, in a precise
spot, and *a beatorum sede distincto*, different from the place
of the chosen. To imagine anything else would be sinister. In the fiftieth chapter of his *History*, Gibbon tries to
diminish Hell's wonders and writes that the two populist
ingredients of fire and darkness are enough to create a
sensation of pain, which can then be infinitely aggravated
by the idea of endless duration. This disgruntled objection
proves perhaps that it is easy to design hell, but it does not
mitigate the admirable terror of its invention. The attribute
of eternity is what is horrible. The continuity – the fact
that divine persecution knows no pause, that there is no
sleep in Hell – is unimaginable. The eternity of that pain,
however, is debatable.

There are two important and beautiful arguments that
invalidate that eternity. The oldest is that of conditional
immortality or annihilation. Immortality, according to its
comprehensive logic, is not an attribute of fallen human
nature, but of God's gift in Christ. It therefore cannot be

1. Nevertheless, the *amateur* of hells would do well not to ignore these
honorable infractions: the Sabian hell, whose four superimposed halls
admit threads of dirty water on the floor, but whose principal room is
vast, dusty, and deserted; Swedenborg's hell, whose gloom is not perceived by the damned who have rejected heaven; Bernard Shaw's hell,
in *Man and Superman*, which attempts to distract its inhabitants from
eternity with the artifices of luxury, art, eroticism, and fame.

used against the same individual upon whom it has been bestowed. It is not a curse but a gift. Whoever merits it, merits heaven; whoever proves unworthy of receiving it, 'dies in death,' as Bunyan wrote, dies without remains. Hell, according to this pious theory, is the blasphemous human name for the denial of God. One of its propounders was Whately, the author of that oft-remembered booklet *Historic Doubts Relative to Napoleon Bonaparte*.

A more curious speculation was presented by the evangelical theologian Rothe, in 1869. His argument – also ennobled by the secret mercy of denying infinite punishment for the damned – states that to eternalize punishment is to eternalize Evil. God, he asserts, does not want *that* eternity for His universe. He insists that it is scandalous to imagine that the sinful man and the Devil would forever mock God's benevolent intentions. (For theology, the creation of the world is an act of love. It uses the term *predestination* to mean 'predestined to glory'; condemnation is merely the opposite, a non-choice translated into infernal torment that does not constitute a special act of divine goodness.) He advocates, finally, a declining, dwindling life for sinners. He foresees them roaming the banks of Creation, or the voids of infinite space, barely sustaining themselves with the leftovers of life. He concludes: As the devils are unconditionally distant from God and are unconditionally His enemies, their activity is against the kingdom of God, and they have organized themselves into a diabolical kingdom, which naturally must choose a leader. The head of that demoniacal government – the Devil – must be imagined as changing. The individuals who assume the throne of that kingdom eventually succumb to the ghostliness of their being, but they are succeeded by their diabolical descendants (*Dogmatik* I, 248).

I now reach the most incredible part of my task, the reasons contrived by humanity in favor of an eternal Hell. I will review them in ascending order of significance. The first is of a disciplinary nature: it postulates that the fearfulness of punishment lies precisely in its eternity, and that to place this in doubt undermines the efficacy of the dogma and plays into the Devil's hands. This argument pertains to the police and does not deserve to be refuted. The second argument is written thus: *Suffering should be infinite because so is the sin of offending the majesty of the Lord, an infinite Being.* It has been observed that this evidence proves so much that we can infer that it proves nothing: it proves that there are no venial sins and that all sins are unpardonable. I would like to add that this is a perfect case of Scholastic frivolity and that its trick is the plurality of meanings of the word *infinite*, which applied to the Lord means 'unconditional,' and to suffering means 'perpetual,' and to guilt means nothing that I can understand. Moreover, arguing that an error against God is infinite because He is infinite is like arguing that it is holy because God is, or like thinking that the injuries attributed to a tiger must be striped.

Now the third argument looms over me. It may, perhaps, be written thus: *Heaven and Hell are eternal because the dignity of free will requires them to be so; either our deeds transcend time, or the 'I' is a delusion.* The virtue of this argument is not logic, it is much more: it is entirely dramatic. It imposes a terrible game on us: we are given the terrifying right to perdition, to persist in evil, to reject all access to grace, to fuel the eternal flames, to make God fail in our destiny, to be forever a shadow, *detestabile cum cacodaemonibus consortium* [in the detestable company of the devil]. Your destiny is real, it tells us; eternal damnation and eternal salvation are in your hands: this responsibility is your honor. A sentiment similar to Bunyan's: 'God did not play in convincing me; the Devil did not play in tempting me; neither did I play when I sunk as into the bottomless pit, when the pangs of hell caught hold upon me; neither do I play in relating of them' (*Grace Abounding to the Chief of Sinners*, preface).

I believe that in our unthinkable destiny, ruled by such infamies as bodily pain, every bizarre thing is possible, even the perpetuity of a Hell, but that it is sacrilegious to believe in it.

Postscript. On this page filled with mere information, I can also report a dream. I dreamed I was awakening from another dream – an uproar of chaos and cataclysms – into an unrecognizable room. Day was dawning: light suffused the room, outlining the foot of the wrought-iron bed, the upright chair, the closed door and windows, the bare table. I thought fearfully, 'Where am I?' and I realized I didn't know. I thought, 'Who am I?' and I couldn't recognize myself. My fear grew. I thought: This desolate awakening is in Hell, this eternal vigil will be my destiny. Then I really woke up, trembling.

[1929]

14

A Defense of Basilides the False

In about 1905, I knew that the omniscient pages (*A to All*) of the first volume of Montaner and Simón's *Hispano-American Encyclopedic Dictionary* contained a small and alarming drawing of a sort of king, with the profiled head of a rooster, a virile torso with open arms brandishing a shield and a whip, and the rest merely a coiled tail, which served as a throne. In about 1916, I read an obscure passage in Quevedo: 'There was the accursed Basilides the heresiarch. There was Nicholas of Antioch, Carpocrates and Cerinthus and the infamous Ebion. Later came Valentinus, he who believed sea and silence to be the beginning of everything.' In about 1923, in Geneva, I came across some heresiological book in German, and I realized that the fateful drawing represented a certain miscellaneous god that was horribly worshiped by the very same Basilides. I also learned what desperate and admirable men the Gnostics were, and I began to study their passionate speculations. Later I was able to investigate the scholarly books of Mead (in the German version: *Fragmente eines verschollenen Glaubens*, 1902) and Wolfgang Schultz (*Dokumente der Gnosis*, 1910), and the articles by Wilhelm Bousset in the *Encyclopedia Britannica*. Today I would like to summarize and illustrate one of their cosmogonies: precisely that of Basilides the heresiarch. I follow entirely the account given by Irenaeus. I realize that many doubt its accuracy, but I suspect that this disorganized revision of musty dreams may in itself be a dream that never inhabited any dreamer. Moreover, the Basilidean heresy is quite simple in form. He was born in Alexandria, they say a hundred years after the Cross, they say among the Syrians and the Greeks. Theology, then, was a popular passion.

In the beginning of Basilides' cosmogony there is a God. This divinity majestically lacks a name, as well as an origin; thus his approximate name, *pater innatus*. His medium is the *pleroma* or plenitude, the inconceivable museum of Platonic archetypes, intelligible essences, and universals. He is an immutable God, but from his repose emanated seven subordinate divinities who, condescending to action, created and presided over a first heaven. From this first demiurgic crown came a second, also with angels, powers, and thrones, and these formed another, lower heaven, which was the symmetrical duplicate of the first. This second conclave saw itself reproduced in a third, and that in another below, and so on down to 365. The lord of the lowest heaven is the God of the Scriptures, and his fraction of divinity is nearly zero. He and his angels founded this visible sky, amassed the immaterial earth on which we are walking, and later apportioned it. Rational oblivion has erased the precise fables this cosmogony attributes to the origin of mankind, but the example of other contemporary imaginations allows us to salvage something, in however vague and speculative a form. In the fragment published by Hilgenfeld, darkness and light had always coexisted, unaware of each other, and when they finally saw each other, light looked and turned away, but darkness, enamored, seized its reflection or memory, and that was the beginning of mankind. In the similar system of Satornilus, heaven grants the worker-angels a momentary vision, and man is fabricated in its likeness, but he drags himself along the ground like a viper until the Lord, in pity, sends him a spark of his power. What is important is what is common to these narratives: our rash or guilty improvisation out of unproductive matter by a deficient divinity. I return to Basilides' history. Cast down by the troublesome angels of the Hebrew God, low humanity deserved the pity of the timeless God, who sent it a redeemer. He was to assume an illusory body, for the flesh degrades. His impassive phantasm hung publicly on the cross, but the essence of Christ passed through the superimposed heavens and was restored to the *pleroma*. He passed through them unharmed, for he knew the secret names of their divinities. 'And those who know the truth of this history,' concludes the profession of faith translated by Irenaeus, 'will know themselves free of the power of the princes who built this world. Each heaven has its own name and likewise each angel and lord and each power of the heaven. He who knows their incomparable names will pass through them invisibly and safely, as the redeemer did. And as the Son was not recognized by anyone, neither shall the Gnostic be. And these mysteries shall not be pronounced, but kept in silence. Know them all, that no one shall know thee.'

The numeric cosmogony of the beginning degenerates toward the end into numeric magic: 365 levels of heaven, at 7 powers per heaven, require the improbable retention of 2,555 oral amulets: a language that the years reduced to the precious name of the redeemer, which is Caulacau, and to that of the immobile God, which is Abraxas. Salvation, for this disillusioned heresy, involves a mnemotechnical effort by the dead, much as the torment of the Savior is an optical illusion – two simulacra which mysteriously harmonize with the precarious reality of their world.

To scoff at the fruitless multiplication of nominal angels and reflected symmetrical heavens in that cosmogony is not terribly difficult. Occam's restrictive principle, *'Entia non sunt multiplicanda praeter necessitatem'* [What can be done with fewer is done in vain with more], could be applied – to demolish it. For my part, I believe such rigor to be anachronistic or worthless. The proper conversion of those heavy, wavering symbols is what matters. I see two intentions in them: the first is a commonplace of criticism; the second – which I do not presume to claim as my discovery – has not, until now, been emphasized. I shall begin with the more obvious. It is a quiet resolution of the problem of evil by means of a hypothetical insertion of a gradual series of divinities between the no less hypothetical God and reality. In the system under examination, these derivations of God dwindle and weaken the further they are removed from God, finally reaching the bottom with the abominable powers who scratched out mankind from base matter. In the account of Valentinus – who did *not* claim the sea and silence to be the beginning of everything – a fallen goddess (Achamoth) has, by a shadow, two sons who are the founder of the world and the devil. An intensification of the story is attributed to Simon Magus: that of having rescued Helen of Troy, formerly first-born daughter of God and later condemned by the angels to painful transmigrations, from a sailors' brothel in Tyre.[1] The thirty-three human years of Jesus Christ and his slow extinguishing on the cross were not sufficient expiation for the harsh Gnostics.

There remains to consider the other meaning of those obscure inventions. The dizzying tower of heavens in the Basilidean heresy, the proliferation of its angels, the planetary shadow of the demiurges disrupting earth, the machinations of the inferior circles against the *pleroma*, the dense population, whether inconceivable or nominal, of that vast mythology, also point to the diminution of this world. Not our evil, but our central insignificance, is predicated in them. Like the grandiose sunsets on the plains, the sky is passionate and monumental and the earth is poor. That is the justification for Valentinus' melodramatic cosmogony, which spins an infinite plot of two supernatural brothers who discover each other, a fallen woman, a powerful mock intrigue among the bad angels, and a final marriage. In this melodrama or serial, the creation of the world is a mere aside. An admirable idea: the world imagined as an essentially futile process, like a sideways, lost glimpse of ancient celestial episodes. Creation as a chance act.

1. Helen, dolorous daughter of God. That divine filiation does not exhaust the connections of her legend to that of Christ. To the latter the followers of Basilides assigned an insubstantial body; of the tragic queen it was claimed that only her *eidolon* or simulacrum was carried away to Troy. A beautiful specter redeemed us; another led to battles and Homer. See, for this Helenaic Docetism, Plato's *Phaedrus*, and Andrew Lang, *Adventures among Books*, 237–248.

The project was heroic; orthodox religious sentiment and theology violently repudiated that possibility. The first creation, for them, was a free and necessary act of God. The universe, as St Augustine would have it understood, did not begin in time, but rather simultaneously with it – a judgment which denies all priority to the Creator. Strauss claims as illusory the hypothesis of an initial moment, for that would contaminate with temporality not only the succeeding moments but also the 'precedent' of eternity.

In the first centuries of our era, the Gnostics disputed with the Christians. They were annihilated, but we can imagine their possible victory. Had Alexandria triumphed and not Rome, the bizarre and confused stories that I have summarized would be coherent, majestic, and ordinary. Lines such as Novalis' 'Life is a sickness of the spirit,'[2] or Rimbaud's despairing 'True life is absent; we are not in the world,' would fulminate from the canonical books. Speculations, such as Richter's discarded theory about the stellar origin of life and its chance dissemination on this planet, would know the unconditional approval of pious laboratories. In any case, what better gift can we hope for than to be insignificant? What greater glory for a God than to be absolved of the world?

[1932]

---

2. That dictum – *'Leben ist eine Krankheit des Geistes, ein leidenschaftliches Tun'* – owes its diffusion to Carlyle, who emphasized it in his famous article in the *Foreign Review*, 1829. Not merely a momentary coincidence, but rather an essential rediscovery of the agonies and enlightenments of Gnosticism, is the *Prophetic Books* of William Blake.

The Translators of
The Thousand and One Nights

1. Captain Burton

At Trieste, in 1872, in a palace with damp statues and deficient hygienic facilities, a gentleman on whose face an African scar told its tale – Captain Richard Francis Burton, the English consul – embarked on a famous translation of the *Quitab alif laila ua laila*, which the *roumis* know by the title *The Thousand and One Nights*. One of the secret aims of his work was the annihilation of another gentleman (also weatherbeaten, and with a dark and Moorish beard) who was compiling a vast dictionary in England and who died long before he was annihilated by Burton. That gentleman was Edward Lane, the Orientalist, author of a highly scrupulous version of *The Thousand and One Nights* that had supplanted a version by Galland. Lane translated against Galland, Burton against Lane; to understand Burton we must understand this hostile dynasty.

I shall begin with the founder. As is known, Jean Antoine Galland was a French Arabist who came back from Istanbul with a diligent collection of coins, a monograph on the spread of coffee, a copy of the *Nights* in Arabic, and a supplementary Maronite whose memory was no less inspired than Scheherazade's. To this obscure consultant – whose name I do not wish to forget: it was Hanna, they say – we owe certain fundamental tales unknown to the original: the stories of Aladdin; the Forty Thieves; Prince Ahmad and the Fairy Peri-Banu; Abu al-Hassan, the Sleeper and the Waker; the night adventure of Caliph Harun al-Rashid; the two sisters who envied their younger sister. The mere mention of these names amply demonstrates that Galland established the canon, incorporating stories that time would render indispensable and that the translators to come – his enemies – would not dare omit.

Another fact is also undeniable. The most famous and eloquent encomiums of *The Thousand and One Nights* – by Coleridge, Thomas De Quincey, Stendhal, Tennyson, Edgar Allan Poe, Newman – are from readers of Galland's translation. Two hundred years and ten better translations have passed, but the man in Europe or the Americas who thinks of *The Thousand and One Nights* thinks, invariably, of this first translation. The Spanish adjective *milyunanochesco* [thousand-and-one-nights-esque] – *milyunanochero* is too Argentine, *milyunanocturno* overly variant – has nothing to do with the erudite obscenities of Burton or Mardrus, and everything to do with Antoine Galland's bijoux and sorceries.

Word for word, Galland's version is the most poorly written of them all, the least faithful, and the weakest, but it was the most widely read. Those who grew intimate with it experienced happiness and astonishment. Its Orientalism, which seems frugal to us now, was bedazzling to men who took snuff and composed tragedies in five acts. Twelve exquisite volumes appeared from 1707 to 1717, twelve volumes that were innumerably read and that passed into various languages, including Hindi and Arabic. We, their mere anachronistic readers of the twentieth century, perceive only the cloying flavor of the eighteenth century in them and not the evaporated aroma of the Orient which two hundred years ago was their novelty and their glory. No one is to blame for this disjunction, Galland least of all. At times, shifts in the language work against him. In the preface to a German translation of *The Thousand and One Nights*, Dr Weil recorded that the merchants of the inexcusable Galland equip themselves with a 'valise full of dates' each time the tale obliges them to cross the desert. It could be argued that in 1710 the mention of dates alone sufficed to erase the image of a valise, but that is unnecessary: *valise*, then, was a sub-species of saddlebag.

There have been other attacks. In a befuddled pane-gyric that survives in his 1921 *Morceaux choisis*, André Gide vituperates the licenses of Antoine Galland, all the better to erase (with a candor that entirely surpasses his reputation) the notion of the literalness of Mardrus, who is as *fin de siècle* as Galland is eighteenth-century, and much more unfaithful.

Galland's discretions are urbane, inspired by decorum, not morality. I copy down a few lines from the third page of his *Nights*: '*Il alla droit a l'appartement de cette princesse, qui, ne s'attendant pas à le revoir, avait reçu dans son lit un des derniers officiers de sa maison*' [He went directly to the chamber of that princess, who, not expecting to see him again, had received in her bed one of the lowliest serv-ants of his household]. Burton concretizes this nebulous *officier*: 'a black cook of loathsome aspect and foul with kitchen grease and grime.' Each, in his way, distorts: the original is less ceremonious than Galland and less greasy than Burton. (Effects of decorum: in Galland's measured prose, *'recevoir dans son lit'* has a brutal ring.)

Ninety years after Antoine Galland's death, an alternate translator of the *Nights* is born: Edward Lane. His biographers never fail to repeat that he is the son of Dr Theophilus Lane, a Hereford prebendary. This generative datum (and the terrible Form of holy cow that it evokes) may be all we need. The Arabized Lane lived five studious years in Cairo, 'almost exclusively among Muslims, speaking and listening to their language, conforming to their customs with the greatest care, and received by all of them as an equal.' Yet neither the high Egyptian nights nor the black and opulent coffee with cardamom seed nor the frequent literary discussions with the Doctors of the Law nor the venerable muslin turban nor the meals eaten with his fingers made him forget his British reticence, the delicate central solitude of the masters of the earth. Consequently, his exceedingly erudite version of the *Nights* is (or seems to be) a mere encyclopedia of evasion. The original is not professionally obscene; Galland corrects occasional indelicacies because he believes them to be in bad taste. Lane seeks them out and persecutes them like an inquisitor. His probity makes no pact with silence: he prefers an alarmed chorus of notes in a cramped supplementary volume, which murmur things like: *I shall overlook an episode of the most reprehensible sort; I suppress a repugnant explanation; Here, a line far too coarse for translation; I must of necessity suppress the other anecdote; Hereafter, a series of omissions; Here, the story of the slave Bujait, wholly inappropriate for translation.* Mutilation does not exclude death: some tales are rejected in their entirety

'because they cannot be purified without destruction.'
This responsible and total repudiation does not strike me
as illogical: what I condemn is the Puritan subterfuge.
Lane is a virtuoso of the subterfuge, an undoubted precursor of the still more bizarre reticences of Hollywood.
My notes furnish me with a pair of examples. In night
391, a fisherman offers a fish to the king of kings, who
wishes to know if it is male or female and is told it is a
hermaphrodite. Lane succeeds in taming this inadmiss-
able colloquy by translating that the king asks what species the fish in question belongs to, and the astute
fisherman replies that it is of a mixed species. The tale of
night 217 speaks of a king with two wives, who lay one
night with the first and the following night with the second, and so they all were happy. Lane accounts for the
good fortune of this monarch by saying that he treated
his wives 'with impartiality.' . . . One reason for this was
that he destined his work for 'the parlor table,' a center
for placid reading and chaste conversation.

The most oblique and fleeting reference to carnal matters is enough to make Lane forget his honor in a pro-
fusion of convolutions and occultations. There is no
other fault in him. When free of the peculiar contact of
this temptation, Lane is of an admirable veracity. He has
no objective, which is a positive advantage. He does not
seek to bring out the barbaric color of the *Nights* like
Captain Burton, or to forget it and attenuate it like Galland, who domesticated his Arabs so they would not be
irreparably out of place in Paris. Lane is at great pains to
be an authentic descendant of Hagar. Galland was completely ignorant of all literal precision; Lane justifies his

interpretation of each problematic word. Galland invoked
an invisible manuscript and a dead Maronite; Lane fur-
nishes editions and page numbers. Galland did not bother
about notes; Lane accumulates a chaos of clarifications
which, in organized form, make up a separate volume. To
be different: this is the rule the precursor imposes. Lane
will follow the rule: he needs only to abstain from abridg-
ing the original.

The beautiful Newman-Arnold exchange (1861–62) –
more memorable than its two interlocutors – extensively
argued the two general ways of translating. Newman
championed the literal mode, the retention of all verbal
singularities: Arnold, the severe elimination of details
that distract or detain. The latter procedure may provide
the charms of uniformity and seriousness; the former,
continuous small surprises. Both are less important than
the translator and his literary habits. To translate the spirit
is so enormous and phantasmal an intent that it may well
be innocuous; to translate the letter, a requirement so
extravagant that there is no risk of its ever being attempted.
More serious than these infinite aspirations is the retention or suppression of certain particularities; more serious than these preferences and oversights is the movement
of the syntax. Lane's syntax is delightful, as befits the
refined parlor table. His vocabulary is often excessively
festooned with Latin words, unaided by any artifice of
brevity. He is careless; on the opening page of his translation he places the adjective *romantic* in the bearded mouth
of a twelfth-century Muslim, which is a kind of futurism.
At times this lack of sensitivity serves him well, for it
allows him to include very commonplace words in a

noble paragraph, with involuntary good results. The most rewarding example of such a cooperation of heterogenous words must be: 'And in this palace is the last information respecting lords collected in the dust.' The following invocation may be another: 'By the Living One who does not die or have to die, in the name of He to whom glory and permanence belong.' In Burton – the occasional precursor of the always fantastical Mardrus – I would be suspicious of so satisfyingly Oriental a formula; in Lane, such passages are so scarce that I must suppose them to be involuntary, in other words, genuine.

The scandalous decorum of the versions by Galland and Lane has given rise to a whole genre of witticisms that are traditionally repeated. I myself have not failed to respect this tradition. It is common knowledge that the two translators did not fulfill their obligation to the unfortunate man who witnessed the Night of Power, to the imprecations of a thirteenth-century garbage collector cheated by a dervish, and to the customs of Sodom. It is common knowledge that they disinfected the *Nights*.

Their detractors argue that this process destroys or wounds the good-hearted naiveté of the original. They are in error; *The Book of the Thousand Nights and a Night* is not (morally) ingenuous; it is an adaptation of ancient stories to the lowbrow or ribald tastes of the Cairo middle classes. Except in the exemplary tales of the *Sindibadnamah*, the indecencies of *The Thousand and One Nights* have nothing to do with the freedom of the paradisiacal state. They are speculations on the part of the editor: their aim is a round of guffaws, their heroes are never more than porters, beggars, or eunuchs. The ancient love stories of the repertory, those which relate cases from the desert or the cities of Arabia, are not obscene, and neither is any production of pre-Islamic literature. They are impassioned and sad, and one of their favorite themes is death for love, the death that an opinion rendered by the *ulamas* declared no less holy than that of a martyr who bears witness to the faith. . . . If we approve of this argument, we may see the timidities of Galland and Lane as the restoration of a primal text.

I know of another defense, a better one. An evasion of the original's erotic opportunities is not an unpardonable sin in the sight of the Lord when the primary aim is to emphasize the atmosphere of magic. To offer mankind a new *Decameron* is a commercial enterprise like so many others; to offer an 'Ancient Mariner,' now, or a '*Bateau ivre*' is a thing that warrants entry into a higher celestial sphere. Littmann observes that *The Thousand and One Nights* is, above all, a repertory of marvels. The universal imposition of this assumption on every Western mind is Galland's work; let there be no doubt on that score. Less fortunate than we, the Arabs claim to think little of the original; they are already well acquainted with the men, mores, talismans, deserts, and demons that the tales reveal to us.

In a passage somewhere in his work, Rafael Cansinos Asséns swears he can salute the stars in fourteen classical and modern languages. Burton dreamed in seventeen languages and claimed to have mastered thirty-five: Semitic, Dravidian, Indo-European, Ethiopic . . . This vast wealth does not complete his definition: it is merely a trait that tallies with the others, all equally excessive. No one was less vulnerable to the frequent gibes in *Hudibras* against learned men who are capable of saying absolutely nothing in several languages. Burton was a man who had a considerable amount to say, and the seventy-two volumes of his complete works say it still. I will note a few titles at random: *Goa and the Blue Mountains* (1851); *A Complete System of Bayonet Exercise* (1853); *Personal Narrative of a Pilgrimage to El-Medinah and Meccah* (1855); *The lake Regions of Central Equatorial Africa* (1860); *The City of the Saints* (1861); *The Highlands of the Brazil* (1869); *On an Hermaphrodite from the Cape de Verde Islands* (1866); *Letters from the Battlefields of Paraguay* (1870); *Ultima Thule* (1875); *To the Gold Coast for Gold* (1883); *The Book of the Sword* (first volume, 1884); *The Perfumed Garden of Cheikh Nefzaoui* – a posthumous work consigned to the flames by Lady Burton, along with the *Priapeia, or the Sporting Epigrams of Divers Poets on Priapus.* The writer can be deduced from this catalogue: the English captain with his passion for geography and for the innumerable ways of being a man that are known to mankind. I will not defame his memory by comparing him to Morand, that sedentary, bilingual gentleman who infinitely ascends and descends in the elevators of identical international hotels, and who pays homage to the sight of a trunk. . . . Burton, disguised as an Afghani, made the pilgrimage to the holy cities of Arabia; his voice begged the Lord to deny his bones and skin, his dolorous flesh and blood, to the Flames of Wrath and Justice; his mouth, dried out by the *samun*, left a kiss on the aerolith that is worshiped in the Kaaba. The adventure is famous: the slightest rumor that an uncircumcised man, a *nasráni*, was profaning the sanctuary would have meant certain death. Before that, in the guise of a dervish, he practiced medicine in Cairo – alternating it with presti-digitation and magic so as to gain the trust of the sick. In 1858, he commanded an expedition to the secret sources of the Nile, a mission that led him to discover Lake Tanganyika. During that undertaking he was attacked by a high fever; in 1855, the Somalis thrust a javelin through his jaws (Burton was coming from Harar, a city in the interior of Abyssinia that was forbidden to Europeans). Nine years later, he essayed the terrible hospitality of the ceremonious cannibals of Dahomey; on his return there was no scarcity of rumors (possibly spread and certainly encouraged by Burton himself) that, like Shakespeare's omnivorous proconsul,[1] he had 'eaten strange flesh.' The Jews, democracy, the British Foreign Office, and Christianity were his preferred objects of loathing; Lord Byron and Islam, his venerations. Of the writer's solitary trade he made

---

1. I allude to Mark Antony, invoked by Caesar's apostrophe: 'On the Alps / It is reported, thou didst eat strange flesh / Which some did die to look on ...' In these lines, I think I glimpse some inverted reflection of the zoological myth of the basilisk, a serpent whose gaze is fatal. Pliny (*Natural History* VIII, par. 33) tells us nothing of the posthumous aptitudes of this ophidian, but the conjunction of the two ideas of seeing (*mirar*) and dying (*morir*) – *'vedi Napoli e poi mori'* [see Naples and die] – must have influenced Shakespeare.

The gaze of the basilisk was poisonous; the Divinity, however, can kill with pure splendor – or pure radiation of *manna*. The direct sight of God is intolerable. Moses covers his face on Mount Horeb, 'for he was afraid to look on God'; Hakim, the prophet of Khorasan, used a four-fold veil of white silk in order not to blind men's eyes Cf. also Isaiah 6:5, and 1 Kings 19:13.

something valiant and plural: he plunged into his work at
dawn, in a vast chamber multiplied by eleven tables, with
the materials for a book on each one – and, on a few, a
bright spray of jasmine in a vase of water. He inspired illustrious friendships and loves: among the former I will name
only that of Swinburne, who dedicated the second series
of *Poems and Ballads* to him – 'in recognition of a friendship which I must always count among the highest hon-
ours of my life' – and who mourned his death in many
stanzas. A man of words and deeds, Burton could well
take up the boast of al-Mutanabbi's *Diwan*:

> The horse, the desert, the night know me,
> Guest and sword, paper and pen.

It will be observed that, from his amateur cannibal to
his dreaming polyglot, I have not rejected those of Richard Burton's personae that, without diminishment of fer-
vor, we could call legendary. My reason is clear: the Burton
of the Burton legend is the translator of the *Nights*. I have
sometimes suspected that the radical distinction between
poetry and prose lies in the very different expectations of
readers: poetry presupposes an intensity that is not tolerated in prose. Something similar happens with Burton's
work: it has a preordained prestige with which no other
Arabist has ever been able to compete. The attractions of
the forbidden are rightfully his. There was a single edition, limited to one thousand copies for the thousand
subscribers of the Burton Club, with a legally binding
commitment never to reprint. (The Leonard C. Smithers
re-edition 'omits given passages in dreadful taste, whose

elimination will be mourned by no one'; Bennett Cerf's representative selection – which purports to be unabridged – proceeds from this purified text.) I will venture a hyperbole: to peruse *The Thousand and One Nights* in Sir Richard's translation is no less incredible than to read it in 'a plain and literal translation with explanatory notes' by Sinbad the Sailor.

The problems Burton resolved are innumerable, but a convenient fiction can reduce them to three: to justify and expand his reputation as an Arabist; to differ from Lane as ostensibly as possible; and to interest nineteenth-century British gentlemen in the written version of thirteenth-century oral Muslim tales. The first of these aims was perhaps incompatible with the third; the second led him into a serious lapse, which I must now disclose. Hundreds of couplets and songs occur in the *Nights*; Lane (incapable of falsehood except with respect to the flesh) translated them precisely into a comfortable prose. Burton was a poet: in 1880 he had privately published *The Kasidah of Haji Abdu*, an evolutionist rhapsody that Lady Burton always deemed far superior to FitzGerald's *Rubáiyát*. His rival's 'prosaic' solution did not fail to arouse Burton's indignation, and he opted for a rendering into English verse – a procedure that was unfortunate from the start, since it contradicted his own rule of total literalness. His ear was as greatly offended against as his sense of logic, for it is not impossible that this quatrain is among the best he came up with:

A night whose stars refused to run their course,
A night of those which never seem outworn:

> Like Resurrection-day, of longsome length
> To him that watched and waited for the morn.[2]

And it is entirely possible that this one is not the worst:

> A sun on wand in knoll of sand she showed,
> Clad in her cramoisy-hued chemisette:
> Of her lips honey-dew she gave me drink,
> And with her rosy cheeks quencht fire she set.

I have alluded to the fundamental difference between the original audience of the tales and Burton's club of subscribers. The former were roguish, prone to exaggeration, illiterate, infinitely suspicious of the present, and credulous of remote marvels; the latter were the respectable men of the West End, well equipped for disdain and erudition but not for belly laughs or terror. The first audience appreciated the fact that the whale died when it heard the man's cry; the second, that there had ever been men who lent credence to any fatal capacity of such a cry. The text's marvels – undoubtedly adequate in Kordofan or Bûlâq, where they were offered up as true – ran the risk of seeming rather threadbare in England. (No one requires that the truth be plausible or instantly ingenious: few readers of the *Life and Correspondence of Karl Marx* will indignantly demand the symmetry of Toulet's *Contrerimes* or the severe precision of an acrostic.) To keep

---

2. Also memorable is this variation on the themes of Abulmeca de Ronda and Jorge Manrique: 'Where is the wight who peopled in the past / Hind-land and Sind; and there the tyrant played?'

his subscribers with him, Burton abounded in explanatory notes on 'the manners and customs of Muslim men,' a territory previously occupied by Lane. Clothing, everyday customs, religious practices, architecture, references to history or to the Koran, games, arts, mythology – all had already been elucidated in the inconvenient precursor's three volumes. Predictably, what was missing was the erotic. Burton (whose first stylistic effort was a highly personal account of the brothels of Bengal) was rampantly capable of filling this gap. Among the delinquent delectations over which he lingered, a good example is a certain random note in the seventh volume, which the index wittily entitles *'capotes mélancoliques'* [melancholy French letters]. The *Edinburgh Review* accused him of writing for the sewer; the *Encyclopedia Britannica* declared that an unabridged translation was unacceptable and that Edward Lane's version 'remained unsurpassed for any truly serious use.' Let us not wax too indignant over this obscure theory of the scientific and documentary superiority of expurgation: Burton was courting these animosities. Furthermore, the slightly varying variations of physical love did not entirely consume the attention of his commentary, which is encyclopedic and seditious and of an interest that increases in inverse proportion to its necessity. Thus volume 6 (which I have before me) includes some three hundred notes, among which are the following: a condemnation of jails and a defense of corporal punishment and fines; some examples of the Islamic respect for bread; a legend about the hairiness of Queen Belkis' legs; an enumeration of the four colors that are emblematic of death; a theory and practice of

Oriental ingratitude; the information that angels prefer a piebald mount, while Djinns favor horses with a bright bay coat; a synopsis of the mythology surrounding the secret Night of Power or Night of Nights; a denunciation of the superficiality of Andrew Lang; a diatribe against rule by democracy; a census of the names of Mohammed, on Earth, in the Fire, and in the Garden; a mention of the Amalekite people, of long years and large stature; a note on the private parts of the Muslim, which for the man extend from the navel to his knees, and for the woman from the top of the head to the tips of her toes; a consideration of the *asa'o* [roasted beef] of the Argentine gaucho; a warning about the discomforts of 'equitation' when the steed is human; an allusion to a grandiose plan for cross-breeding baboons with women and thus deriving a sub-race of good proletarians. At fifty, a man has accumulated affections, ironies, obscenities, and copious anecdotes; Burton unburdened himself of them in his notes.

The basic problem remains: how to entertain nineteenth-century gentlemen with the pulp fictions of the thirteenth century? The stylistic poverty of the *Nights* is well known. Burton speaks somewhere of the 'dry and business-like tone' of the Arab prosifiers, in contrast to the rhetorical luxuriance of the Persians. Littmann, the ninth translator, accuses himself of having interpolated words such as *asked*, *begged*, *answered*, in five thousand pages that know of no other formula than an invariable *said*. Burton lovingly abounds in this type of substitution. His vocabulary is as unparalleled as his notes. Archaic words coexist with slang, the lingo of prisoners or sailors with technical terms. He does not shy away from the glorious hybridization of English: neither Morris' Scandinavian repertory nor Johnson's Latin has his blessing, but rather the contact and reverberation of the two. Neologisms and foreignisms are in plentiful supply: *castrato, inconséquence, hauteur, in gloria, bagnio, langue fourée, pundonor, vendetta, Wazir*. Each of these is indubitably the *mot juste*, but their interspersion amounts to a kind of skewing of the original. A good skewing, since such verbal – and syntactical – pranks beguile the occasionally exhausting course of the *Nights*. Burton administers them carefully: first he translates gravely, 'Sulayman, Son of David (on the twain be peace!)'; then – once this majesty is familiar to us – he reduces it to 'Solomon Davidson.' A king who, for the other translators, is 'King of Samarcand in Persia,' is, for Burton, 'King of Samarcand in Barbarianland'; a merchant who, for the others, is 'ill-tempered,' is 'a man of wrath.' That is not all: Burton rewrites in its entirety – with the addition of circumstantial details and physiological traits – the initial and final story. He thus, in 1885, inaugurates a procedure whose perfection (or whose *reductio ad absurdum*) we will now consider in Mardrus. An Englishman is always more timeless than a Frenchman: Burton's heterogenous style is less antiquated than Mardrus', which is noticeably dated.

2. Doctor Mardrus

Mardrus' destiny is a paradoxical one. To him has been ascribed the *moral* virtue of being the most truthful translator of *The Thousand and One Nights*, a book of admirable lascivity, whose purchasers were previously hoodwinked by Galland's good manners and Lane's Puritan qualms. His prodigious literalness, thoroughly demonstrated by the inarguable subtitle 'Literal and complete translation of the Arabic text,' is revered, along with the inspired idea of writing *The Book of the Thousand Nights and One Night*. The history of this title is instructive; we should review it before proceeding with our investigation of Mardrus.

Masudi's *Meadows of Gold and Mines of Precious Stones* describes an anthology titled *Hazar afsana*, Persian words whose true meaning is 'a thousand adventures,' but which people renamed 'a thousand nights.' Another tenth-century document, the *Fihrist*, narrates the opening tale of the series; the king's heartbroken oath that every night he will wed a virgin whom he will have beheaded at dawn, and the resolution of Scheherazade, who diverts him with marvelous stories until a thousand nights have revolved over the two of them and she shows him his son. This invention – far superior to the future and analogous devices of Chaucer's pious cavalcade or Giovanni Boccaccio's epidemic – is said to be posterior to the title, and was devised in the aim of justifying it. . . . Be that as it may, the early figure of 1000 quickly increased to 1001. How did this additional and now indispensable night emerge, this prototype of Pico della Mirandola's *Book of All Things and Also Many Others*, so derided by Quevedo and later Voltaire? Littmann suggests a contamination of the Turkish phrase *'bin bir,'* literally 'a thousand and one,' but commonly used to mean 'many.' In early 1840, Lane advanced a more beautiful reason: the magical dread of even numbers. The title's adventures certainly did not end there. Antoine Galland, in 1704, eliminated the original's repetition and translated *The Thousand and One Nights*, a name now familiar in all the nations of Europe except England, which prefers *The Arabian Nights*. In 1839, the editor of the Calcutta edition, W. H. Macnaghten, had the singular scruple of translating *Quitab alif laila ua laila* as *Book of the Thousand Nights and One Night*. This renovation through spelling did not go unremarked. John Payne, in 1882, began publishing his *Book of the Thousand Nights and One Night*; Captain Burton, in 1885, his *Book of the Thousand Nights and a Night*; J. C. Mardrus, in 1899, his *Livre des mille nuits et une nuit*.

I turn to the passage that made me definitively doubt this last translator's veracity. It belongs to the doctrinal story of the City of Brass, which in all other versions extends from the end of night 566 through part of night 578, but which Dr Mardrus has transposed (for what cause, his Guardian Angel alone knows) to nights 338–346. I shall not insist on this point; we must not waste our consternation on this inconceivable reform of an ideal calendar. Scheherazade-Mardrus relates:

> The water ran through four channels worked in the chamber's floor with charming meanderings, and each channel had a bed of a special color; the first channel had a bed of pink porphyry; the second of topaz, the third of emerald, and the fourth of turquoise; so that the water was tinted the color of the bed, and bathed by the attenuated light filtered in through the silks above, it projected

onto the surrounding objects and the marble walls all the sweetness of a seascape.

As an attempt at visual prose in the manner of *The Portrait of Dorian Gray*, I accept (and even salute) this description; as a 'literal and complete' version of a passage composed in the thirteenth century, I repeat that it alarms me unendingly. The reasons are multiple. A Scheherazade without Mardrus describes by enumerating parts, not by mutual reaction; does not attest to circumstantial details like that of water that takes on the color of its bed; does not define the quality of light filtered by silk; and does not allude to the Salon des Aquarellistes in the final image. Another small flaw: 'charming meanderings' is not Arabic, it is very distinctly French. I do not know if the foregoing reasons are sufficient; they were not enough for me, and I had the indolent pleasure of comparing the three German versions by Weil, Henning, and Littmann, and the two English versions by Lane and Sir Richard Burton. In them I confirmed that the original of Mardrus' ten lines was this: 'The four drains ran into a fountain, which was of marble in various colors.'

Mardrus' interpolations are not uniform. At times they are brazenly anachronistic – as if suddenly Marchand's withdrawal were being discussed. For example:

They were overlooking a dream city. . . . As far as the gaze fixed on horizons drowned by the night could reach, the vale of bronze was terraced with the cupolas of palaces, the balconies of houses, and serene gardens; canals illuminated by the moon ran in a thousand clear circuits in the shadow of the peaks, while away in the distance, a sea of metal contained the sky's reflected fires in its cold bosom.

Or this passage, whose Gallicism is no less public:

A magnificent carpet of glorious colors and dexterous wool opened its odorless flowers in a meadow without sap, and lived all the artificial life of its verdant groves full of birds and animals, surprised in their exact natural beauty and their precise lines.

(Here the Arabic editions state: 'To the sides were carpets, with a variety of birds and beasts embroidered in red gold and white silver, but with eyes of pearls and rubies. Whoever saw them could not cease to wonder at them.')

Mardrus cannot cease to wonder at the poverty of the 'Oriental color' of *The Thousand and One Nights*. With a stamina worthy of Cecil B. de Mille, he heaps on the viziers, the kisses, the palm trees, and the moons. He happens to read, in night 570:

They arrived at a column of black stone, in which a man was buried up to his armpits. He had two enormous wings and four arms; two of which were like the arms of the sons of Adam, and two like a lion's forepaws, with iron claws. The hair on his head was like a horse's tail, and his eyes were like embers, and he had in his forehead a third eye which was like the eye of a lynx.

He translates luxuriantly:

> One evening the caravan came to a column of black stone, to which was chained a strange being, only half of whose body could be seen, for the other half was buried in the ground. The bust that emerged from the earth seemed to be some monstrous spawn riveted there by the force of the infernal powers. It was black and as large as the trunk of an old, rotting palm tree, stripped of its fronds. It had two enormous black wings and four hands, of which two were like the clawed paws of a lion. A tuft of coarse bristles like a wild ass's tail whipped wildly over its frightful skull. Beneath its orbital arches flamed two red pupils, while its double-horned forehead was pierced by a single eye, which opened, immobile and fixed, shooting out green sparks like the gaze of a tiger or a panther.

Somewhat later he writes:

> The bronze of the walls, the fiery gemstones of the cupolas, the ivory terraces, the canals and all the sea, as well as the shadows projected towards the West, merged harmoniously beneath the nocturnal breeze and the magical moon.

'Magical,' for a man of the thirteenth century, must have been a very precise classification, and not the gallant doctor's mere urbane adjective. . . . I suspect that the Arabic language is incapable of a 'literal and complete' version of Mardrus' paragraph, and neither is Latin or the Spanish of Miguel de Cervantes.

The Book of the Thousand and One Nights abounds in two procedures: one (purely formal), rhymed prose; the other, moral predications. The first, retained by Burton and by Littmann, coincides with the narrator's moments of animation: people of comely aspect, palaces, gardens, magical operations, mentions of the Divinity, sunsets, battles, dawns, the beginnings and endings of tales. Mardrus, perhaps mercifully, omits it. The second requires two faculties: that of majestically combining abstract words and that of offering up stock comments without embarrassment. Mardrus lacks both. From the line memorably translated by Lane as 'And in this palace is the last information respecting lords collected in the dust,' the good Doctor barely extracts: 'They passed on, all of them! They had barely the time to repose in the shadow of my towers.' The angel's confession – 'I am imprisoned by Power, confined by Splendor, and punished for as long as the Eternal commands it, to whom Force and Glory belong' – is, for Mardrus' reader, 'I am chained here by the Invisible Force until the extinction of the centuries.'

Nor does sorcery have in Mardrus a co-conspirator of good will. He is incapable of mentioning the supernatural without smirking. He feigns to translate, for example:

One day when Caliph Abdelmelik, hearing tell of certain vessels of antique copper whose contents were a strange black smoke-cloud of diabolical form, marveled greatly and seemed to place in doubt the reality of facts so commonly known, the traveller Talib ben-Sahl had to intervene.

In this paragraph (like the others I have cited, it belongs to the Story of the City of Brass, which, in Mardrus, is made of imposing Bronze), the deliberate candor of 'so commonly known' and the rather implausible doubts of Caliph Abdelmelik are two personal contributions by the translator.

Mardrus continually strives to complete the work neglected by those languid, anonymous Arabs. He adds Art Nouveau passages, fine obscenities, brief comical interludes, circumstantial details, symmetries, vast quantities of visual Orientalism. An example among so many: in night 573, the Emir Musa bin Nusayr orders his blacksmiths and carpenters to construct a strong ladder of wood and iron. Mardrus (in his night 344) reforms this dull episode, adding that the men of the camp went in search of dry branches, peeled them with knives and scimitars, and bound them together with turbans, belts, camel ropes, leather cinches, and tack, until they had built a tall ladder that they propped against the wall, supporting it with stones on both sides. . . . In general, it can be said that Mardrus does not translate the book's words but its scenes: a freedom denied to translators, but tolerated in illustrators, who are allowed to add these kinds of details. . . . I do not know if these smiling diversions are what infuse the work with such a happy air, the air of a far-fetched personal yarn rather than of a laborious hefting of dictionaries. But to me the Mardrus 'translation' is the most readable of them all – after Burton's incomparable version, which is not truthful either. (In Burton, the falsification is of another order. It resides in the gigantic employ of a gaudy English, crammed with archaic and barbaric words.)

I would greatly deplore it (not for Mardrus, for myself) if any constabulary intent were read into the foregoing scrutiny. Mardrus is the only Arabist whose glory was promoted by men of letters, with such unbridled success that even the Arabists still know who he is. André Gide was among the first to praise him, in August, 1889; I do not think Cancela and Capdevila will be the last. My aim is not to demolish this admiration but to substantiate it. To celebrate Mardrus' fidelity is to leave out the soul of Mardrus, to ignore Mardrus entirely. It is his infidelity, his happy and creative infidelity, that must matter to us.

3. Enno Littmann

Fatherland to a famous Arabic edition of *The Thousand and One Nights*, Germany can take (vain) glory in four versions: by the 'librarian though Israelite' Gustav Weil – the adversative is from the Catalan pages of a certain encyclopedia –; by Max Henning, translator of the Koran; by the man of letters Félix Paul Greve; and by Enno Littmann, decipherer of the Ethiopic inscriptions in the fortress of Axum. The first of these versions, in four volumes (1839–42), is the most pleasurable, as its author – exiled from Africa and Asia by dysentery – strives to maintain or substitute for the Oriental style. His interpolations earn my deepest respect. He has some intruders at a gathering say, 'We do not wish to be like the morning, which disperses all revelries.' Of a generous king, he assures us, 'The fire that burns for his guests brings to mind the Inferno and the dew of his benign hand is like the Deluge'; of another he tells us that his hands 'were liberal as the sea.' These fine apocrypha are not unworthy of Burton or Mardrus, and the translator assigned them to the parts in verse, where this graceful animation can be an *ersatz* or replacement for the original rhymes. Where the prose is concerned, I see that he translated it as is, with certain justified omissions, equidistant from hypocrisy and immodesty. Burton praised his work – 'as faithful as a translation of a popular nature can be.' Not in vain was Dr Weil Jewish, 'though librarian'; in his language I think I perceive something of the flavor of Scripture.

The second version (1895–97) dispenses with the enchantments of accuracy, but also with those of style. I am speaking of the one provided by Henning, a Leipzig Arabist, to Philippe Reclam's *Universalbibliothek*. This is an expurgated version, though the publisher claims otherwise. The style is dogged and flat. Its most indisputable virtue must be its length. The editions of Bûlâq and Breslau are represented, along with the Zotenberg manuscripts and Burton's *Supplemental Nights*. Henning, translator of Sir Richard, is, word for word, superior to Henning, translator of Arabic, which is merely a confirmation of Sir Richard's primacy over the Arabs. In the book's preface and conclusion, praises of Burton abound – almost

45

deprived of their authority by the information that Burton wielded 'the language of Chaucer, equivalent to medieval Arabic.' A mention of Chaucer as *one* of the sources of Burton's vocabulary would have been more reasonable. (Another is Sir Thomas Urquhart's Rabelais.)

The third version, Greve's, derives from Burton's English and repeats it, excluding only the encyclopedic notes. Insel-Verlag published it before the war.

The fourth (1923–28) comes to supplant the previous one and, like it, runs to six volumes. It is signed by Enno Littmann, decipherer of the monuments of Axum, cataloguer of the 283 Ethiopic manuscripts found in Jerusalem, contributor to the *Zeitschrift für Assyriologie.* Though it does not engage in Burton's indulgent loitering, Littmann's translation is entirely frank. The most ineffable obscenities do not give him pause; he renders them into his placid German, only rarely into Latin. He omits not a single word, not even those that register – 1000 times – the passage from one night to the next. He neglects or refuses all local color: express instructions from the publisher were necessary to make him retain the name of Allah and not substitute it with God. Like Burton and John Payne, he translates Arabic verse into Western verse. He notes ingenuously that if the ritual announcement 'So-and-so pronounced these verses' were followed by a paragraph of German prose, his readers would be disconcerted. He provides whatever notes are necessary for a basic understanding of the text: twenty or so per volume, all of them laconic. He is always lucid, readable, mediocre. He follows (he tells us) the very breath of the Arabic. If the *Encyclopedia Britannica* contains no errors, his translation is the best of all those in circulation. I hear that the Arabists agree; it matters not at all that a mere man of letters – and he of the merely Argentine Republic – prefers to dissent.

My reason is this: the versions by Burton and Mardrus, and even by Galland, can only be conceived of *in the wake of a literature.* Whatever their blemishes or merits, these characteristic works presuppose a rich (prior) process. In some way, the almost inexhaustible process of English is adumbrated in Burton – John Donne's hard obscenity, the gigantic vocabularies of Shakespeare and Cyril Tourneur, Swinburne's affinity for the archaic, the crass erudition of the authors of 17th-century chapbooks, the energy and imprecision, the love of tempests and magic. In Mardrus' laughing paragraphs, *Salammbô* and La Fontaine, the *Mannequin d'osier* and the *ballets russes* all coexist. In Littmann, who like Washington cannot tell a lie, there is nothing but the probity of Germany. This is so little, so very little. The commerce between Germany and the *Nights* should have produced something more.

Whether in philosophy or in the novel, Germany possesses a literature of the fantastic – rather, it possesses *only* a literature of the fantastic. There are marvels in the *Nights* that I would like to see rethought in German. As I formulate this desire, I think of the repertory's deliberate wonders – the all-powerful slaves of a lamp or a ring; Queen Lab, who transforms Muslims into birds; the copper boatman with talismans and formulae on his chest – and of those more general ones that proceed from its collective nature, from the need to complete one thousand and one episodes. Once they had run out of magic, the copyists had to fall back on historical or pious notices whose inclusion seems to attest to the good faith of the rest. The ruby that ascends into the sky and the earliest description of Sumatra, details of the court of the Abbasids and silver angels whose food is the justification of the Lord, all dwell together in a single volume. It is, finally, a poetic mixture; and I would say the same of certain repetitions. Is it not portentous that on night 602 King Schahriah hears his own story from the queen's lips? Like the general framework, a given tale often contains within itself other tales of equal length: stages within the stage as in the tragedy of *Hamlet*, raised to the power of a dream. A clear and difficult line from Tennyson seems to define them:

Laborious orient ivory, sphere in sphere.

To further heighten the astonishment, these adventitious Hydra's heads can be more concrete than the body: Schahriah, the fantastical king 'of the Islands of China and Hindustan,' receives news of Tarik ibn Ziyad, governor of Tangiers and victor in the battle of Guadalete. . . . The threshold is confused with the mirror, the mask lies beneath the face, no one knows any longer which is the true man and which are his idols. And none of it matters; the disorder is as acceptable and trivial as the inventions of a daydream.

Chance has played at symmetries, contrasts, digressions. What might a man – a Kafka – do if he organized and intensified this play, remade it in line with the Germanic distortion, the *unheimlichkeit* of Germany?

[1934–1936]

Among the volumes consulted, I must enumerate:

Les Mille et une Nuits, contes arabes traduits par Galland. Paris, s.d.

The Thousand and One Nights, commonly called The Arabian Nights' Entertainments. A new translation from the Arabic by E.W. Lane. London, 1839.

The Book of the Thousand Nights and a Night. A plain and literal translation by Richard F. Burton. London (?) n.d. Vols. VI, VII, VIII.

The Arabian Nights. A complete [sic] *and unabridged selection from the famous literal translation of R. F. Burton.* New York, 1932.

Le Livre des mille nuits et une nuit. Traduction littérale et complète du texte arabe par le Dr J. C. Mardrus. Paris, 1906.

Tausend und eine Nacht. Aus dem Arabischen übertragen von Max Henning. Leipzig 1897.

Die Erzählungen aus den Tausendundein Nächten. Nach dem arabischen Urtext der Calcuttaer Ausgabe vom Jahre 1839 übertragen von Enno Littmann. Leipzig, 1928.

The Labyrinths of the Detective Story and Chesterton

The English live with the turmoil of two incompatible passions: a strange appetite for adventure and a strange appetite for legality. I write 'strange' because, for a *criollo*, they are both precisely that. Martín Fierro, the sainted army deserter, and his pal Cruz, the sainted police deserter, would be astonished, swearing and laughing at the British (and American) doctrine that the law is infallibly right; yet they would never dare to imagine that their miserable fate as cutthroats was interesting or desirable. For a *criollo*, to kill is to 'disgrace oneself.' It is one of man's misfortunes, and in itself neither grants nor diminishes virtue. Nothing could be more opposite to 'Murder Considered as One of the Fine Arts' by the 'morbidly virtuous' De Quincey or to the 'Theory of the Moderate Murder' by the sedentary Chesterton.

Both passions – for physical adventure and for rancorous legality – find satisfaction in the current detective narrative. Its prototypes are the old serials and current dime novels about the nominally famous Nick Carter, smiling and hygienic athlete, that were engendered by the journalist John Coryell on an insomniac typewriter that dispatched 70,000 words a month. The genuine detective story – need I say it? – rejects with equal disdain both physical risk and distributive justice. It serenely disregards jails, secret stairways, remorse, gymnastics, fake beards, fencing, Charles Baudelaire's bats, and even the element of chance. In the earliest examples of the genre ('The Mystery of Marie Rogêt,' by Edgar Allan Poe, 1842) and in one of the most recent ones (*Unravelled Knots*, by the Baroness Orczy), the story is limited to the discussion and abstract resolution of a crime, often far from the event or many years after it. The everyday methods of police investigation – fingerprints, torture, accusation – would seem like solecisms there. One might object to the conventionality of this rejection, but the convention here is irreproachable: it does not attempt to avoid difficulties, but rather to impose them. It is not a convenience for the writer, like the confused confidants in Jean Racine or theatrical asides. The detective novel to some degree borders on the psychological novel (*The Moonstone* by Wilkie Collins, 1868; *Mr Digweed and Mr Lumb* by Eden Phillpotts, 1934). The short story is of a strict, problematic nature; its code could be the following:

A.) *A discretional limit of six characters.* The reckless infraction of this law is responsible for the confusion and tedium of all detective movies. In every one we are presented with fifteen strangers, and it is finally revealed that the evil one is not Alpha, who was looking through the keyhole, nor Beta, who hid the money, nor the disturbing Gamma, who would sob in the corners of the hallway, but rather that surly young Upsilon, whom we'd been confusing with Phi, who bears such a striking resemblance to Tau, the substitute elevator operator. The astonishment this fact tends to produce is somewhat moderate.

B.) *The declaration of all the terms of the problem.* If my memory (or lack of it) serves me, the varied infraction of this second law is the favorite defect of Conan Doyle. It involves, at times, a few particles of ashes, gathered behind the reader's back by the privileged Holmes, and only derivable from a cigar made in Burma, which is sold in only one store, which is patronized by only one customer. At other times, the cheating is more serious. It involves a guilty party, horribly unmasked at the last moment, who turns out to be a stranger, an insipid and torpid interpolation. In honest stories, the criminal is one of the characters present from the beginning.

C.) *An avaricious economy of means.* The final discovery that two characters in the plot are the same person may be appealing – as long as the instrument of change turns out to be not a false beard or an Italian accent, but different names and circumstances. The less delightful version – two individuals who imitate a third and thus provide him with ubiquity – runs the certain risk of heavy weather.

D.) *The priority of how over who.* The amateurs I excoriated in section A are partial to the story of a jewel placed within the reach of fifteen men – that is, of fifteen names, because we know nothing about their characters – which then disappears into the heavy fist of one of them. They imagine that the act of ascertaining to which name the fist belongs is of considerable interest.

E.) *A reticence concerning death.* Homer could relate that a sword severed the hand of Hypsenor and that the bloody hand rolled over the ground and that blood-red death and cruel fate seized his eyes; such displays are inappropriate in the detective story, whose glacial muses are hygiene, fallacy, and order.

F.) *A solution that is both necessary and marvelous.* The

former establishes that the problem is a 'determined' one, with only one solution. The latter requires that the solution be something that the reader marvels over – without, of course, resorting to the supernatural, whose use in this genre of fiction is slothful and felonious. Also prohibited are hypnotism, telepathic hallucinations, portents, elixirs with unknown effects, ingenious pseudoscientific tricks, and lucky charms. Chesterton always performs a *tour de force* by proposing a supernatural explanation and then replacing it, losing nothing, with one from this world.

The Scandal of Father Brown, Chesterton's most recent book (London, 1935), has suggested the aforementioned rules. Of the five series of chronicles of the little clergyman, this book is probably the least felicitous. It contains, however, two stories that I would not want excluded from a Brownian anthology or canon: the third, 'The Blast of the Book' and the eighth, 'The Insoluble Problem.' The premise of the former is exciting: it deals with a tattered supernatural book that causes the instantaneous disappearance of those who foolishly open it. Somebody announces over the telephone that he has the book in front of him and that he is about to open it; the frightened listener 'hears a kind of silent explosion.' Another exploded character leaves a small hole in a pane of glass; another, a rip in a canvas; another, his abandoned wooden leg. The *dénouement* is good, but I am positive that the most devout readers correctly guessed it in the middle of page 73. There is an abundance of the characteristics typical of G. K.: for example, that gloomy masked man with the black gloves who turns out to be an aristocrat and a fierce opponent of nudism.

The settings for the crimes are remarkable, as in all of Chesterton's books, and carefully and sensationally false. Has anyone ever noted the similarities between the fantastic London of Stevenson and that of Chesterton, between the mourning gentlemen and nocturnal gardens of *The Suicide Club* and those of the now five-part saga of Father Brown?

[1935]

Two Films (*Crime and Punishment* and *The Thirty-Nine Steps*)

One is called *Crime and Punishment*, by Dostoevsky / von Sternberg. The fact that the first collaborator – the deceased Russian – has not actually collaborated will alarm no one, given the practices of Hollywood; that any trace left by the second – the dreamy Viennese – is equally unnoticeable borders on the monstrous. I can understand how the 'psychological' novel might not interest a man, or might not interest him any longer. I could imagine that von Sternberg, devoted to the inexorable Muse of Bric-à-Brac, might reduce all the mental (or at least feverish) complexities of Rodion Romanovich's crime to the depiction of a pawnbroker's house crammed with intolerable objects, or a police station resembling Hollywood's notion of a Cossack barracks. Indoctrinated by the populous memory of *The Scarlet Empress*, I was expecting a vast flood of false beards, miters, samovars, masks, surly faces, wrought-iron gates, vineyards, chess pieces, balalaikas, prominent cheekbones, and horses. In short, I was expecting the usual von Sternberg nightmare, the suffocation and the madness. All in vain! In this film, von Sternberg has discarded his usual caprices, which could be an excellent omen, but unfortunately, he has not replaced them with anything. Without transition or pause, he has merely passed from a hallucinatory state (*The Scarlet Empress*, *The Devil Is a Woman*) to a foolish state. Formerly he seemed mad, which at least was something; now he seems merely simple-minded. Nevertheless, there is no cause for despair: perhaps *Crime and Punishment*, a totally vacuous work, is a sign of remorse and penitence, a necessary act of purification. Perhaps *Crime and Punishment* is only a bridge between the vertiginous sound and fury of *The Scarlet Empress* and a forthcoming film that will reject not only the peculiar charms of chaos but will also resemble – once again – intelligence. (In writing 'once again,' I am thinking of Josef von Sternberg's early films.)

From an extraordinarily intense novel, von Sternberg has derived an empty film; from an absolutely dull adventure story – *The Thirty-Nine Steps* by John Buchan – Hitchcock has made a good film. He has invented episodes, inserted wit and mischief where the original contained only heroism. He has thrown in delightfully unsentimental erotic relief, and also a thoroughly charming character, Mr Memory. Infinitely removed from the other two faculties of the mind, this man reveals a grave secret simply because someone asks it of him and because to answer, at that moment, is his role.

[1936]

Joyce's Latest Novel

Work in Progress has appeared at last, now titled *Finnegans Wake*, and is, they tell us, the ripened and lucid fruit of sixteen energetic years of literary labor. I have examined it with some bewilderment, have unenthusiastically deciphered nine or ten *calembours*, and have read the terror-stricken praise in the *N.R.F.* and the *T.L.S.* The trenchant authors of those accolades claim that they have discovered the rules of this complex verbal labyrinth, but they abstain from applying or formulating them; nor do they attempt the analysis of a single line or paragraph. . . . I suspect that they share my essential bewilderment and my useless and partial glances at the text. I suspect that they secretly hope (as I publicly do) for an exegetical treatise from Stuart Gilbert, the official interpreter of James Joyce.

It is unquestionable that Joyce is one of the best writers of our time. Verbally, he is perhaps the best. In *Ulysses* there are sentences, there are paragraphs, that are not inferior to Shakespeare or Sir Thomas Browne. In *Finnegans Wake* itself there are some memorable phrases. (This one, for example, which I will not attempt to translate: 'Beside the rivering waters of, hither and thithering waters of, night.') In this enormous book, however, efficacy is an exception.

Finnegans Wake is a concatenation of puns committed

in a dreamlike English that is difficult not to categorize as frustrated and incompetent. I don't think that I am exaggerating. *Ameise*, in German, means 'ant.' Joyce, in *Work in Progress*, combines it with the English *amazing* to coin the adjective *ameising*, meaning the wonder inspired by an ant. Here is another example, perhaps less lugubrious. Joyce fuses the English words *banister* and *star* into a single word, *banistar*, that combines both images.

Jules Laforgue and Lewis Carroll have played this game with better luck.

[1939]

A Pedagogy of Hatred

Displays of hatred are even more obscene and denigrating than exhibitionism. I defy pornographers to show me a picture more vile than any of the twenty-two illustrations that comprise the children's book *Trau keinem Fuchs auf gruener Heid und keinem Jud bei seinem Eid* [Don't Trust Any Fox from a Heath or Any Jew on his Oath] whose fourth edition now infests Bavaria. It was first published a year ago, in 1936, and has already sold 51,000 copies. Its goal is to instill in the children of the Third Reich a distrust and animosity toward Jews. Verse (we know the mnemonic virtues of rhyme) and color engravings (we know how effective images are) collaborate in this veritable textbook of hatred.

Take any page: for example, page 5. Here I find, not without justifiable bewilderment, this didactic poem – 'The German is a proud man who knows how to work and struggle. Jews detest him because he is so handsome and enterprising' – followed by an equally informative and explicit quatrain: 'Here's the Jew, recognizable to all, the biggest scoundrel in the whole kingdom. He thinks he's wonderful, and he's horrible.' The engravings are more astute: the German is a Scandinavian, eighteen-year-old athlete, plainly portrayed as a worker; the Jew is a dark Turk, obese and middle-aged. Another sophistic feature is that the German is clean-shaven and the Jew, while bald, is very hairy. (It is well known that German Jews are *Ashkenazim*, copper-haired Slavs. In this book they are presented as dark half-breeds so that they'll appear to be the exact opposite of the blond beasts. Their attributes also include the permanent use of a fez, a rolled cigar, and ruby rings.)

Another engraving shows a lecherous dwarf trying to seduce a young German lady with a necklace. In another, the father reprimands his daughter for accepting the gifts and promises of Solly Rosenfeld, who certainly will not make her his wife. Another depicts the foul body odor and shoddy negligence of Jewish butchers. (How could this be, with all the precautions they take to make meat kosher?) Another, the disadvantages of being swindled by a lawyer, who solicits from his clients a constant flow of flour, fresh eggs, and veal cutlets. After a year of this, the clients have lost their case but the Jewish lawyer 'weighs two hundred and forty pounds.' Yet another depicts the opportune expulsion of Jewish professors as a relief for the children: 'We want a German teacher,' shout the enthusiastic pupils, 'a joyful teacher who knows how to play with us and maintain order and discipline. We want a German teacher who will teach us common sense.' It is difficult not to share such aspirations.

What can one say about such a book? Personally I am outraged, less for Israel's sake than for Germany's, less for the offended community than for the offensive nation. I don't know if the world can do without German civilization, but I do know that its corruption by the teachings of hatred is a crime.

[1937]

60

A Comment on August 23, 1944

That crowded day gave me three distinct surprises: the physical degree of joy I felt when they told me that Paris had been liberated; the discovery that a collective emotion can be noble; the puzzling and flagrant enthusiasm of many who were supporters of Hitler. I know that if I question that enthusiasm, I may easily resemble those futile hydrographers who asked why a single ruby was enough to arrest the course of a river; many will accuse me of trying to explain a fantastic event. Still, it happened, and thousands of persons in Buenos Aires can bear witness.

I realized immediately that it was useless to ask those people themselves. They are fickle, and by behaving incoherently they are no longer aware that incoherence need be justified. They adore the German race, but they abhor 'Saxon' America; they condemn the articles of Versailles, but they applaud the wonders of the *Blitzkrieg*; they are anti-Semitic, but they profess a religion of Hebrew origin; they celebrate submarine warfare, but they vigorously condemn British acts of piracy; they denounce imperialism, but they defend and proclaim the theory of *Lebensraum*; they idolize San Martín, but they regard the independence of America as a mistake; they apply the canon of Jesus to the actions of England, but the canon of Zarathustra to those of Germany.

I also reflected that any other uncertainty was prefer-
able to the uncertainty of a dialogue with these siblings
of chaos, exonerated from honor and piety by the infinite
repetition of the interesting formula *I am Argentine.* Furthermore, did Freud not argue and Walt Whitman not
foresee that men have very little knowledge of the real
motives for their conduct? Perhaps, I said to myself, the
magic of the symbols *Paris* and *liberation* is so powerful
that Hitler's partisans have forgotten that the defeat of
his forces is the meaning of those symbols. Wearily, I
chose to imagine that the probable explanation for this
conundrum was their fear, their inconstancy, and their
mere adherence to reality.

Several nights later, I was enlightened by a book and
a memory. The book was Shaw's *Man and Superman*; the
passage in question was John Tanner's metaphysical
dream, where he affirms that the horror of Hell is its unreality. This conviction can be compared with the doctrine
of another Irishman, John Scotus Erigena, who denied the
substantive existence of sin and evil, and declared that all
creatures, including the Devil, will return to God. The
memory was the day that had been the exact and hateful
opposite of August 23, 1944: June 14, 1940. A certain Ger-
manophile, whose name I do not wish to remember,
came to my house that day. Standing in the doorway, he
announced the dreadful news: the Nazi armies had occupied Paris. I felt a confusion of sadness, disgust, malaise.
Then it occurred to me that his insolent joy did not
explain the stentorian voice or the abrupt proclamation.
He added that the German troops would soon be in London. Any opposition was useless, nothing could prevent

their victory. That was when I knew that he, too, was terrified.

I do not know whether the facts I have related require clarification. I believe I can interpret them like this: for Europeans and Americans, one order and only one is possible; it used to be called Rome, and now it is called Western Culture. To be a Nazi (to play the energetic barbarian, Viking, Tartar, sixteenth-century conquistador, gaucho, or Indian) is, after all, mentally and morally impossible. Nazism suffers from unreality, like Erigena's hell. It is uninhabitable; men can only die for it, lie for it, wound and kill for it. No one, in the intimate depths of his being, can wish it to triumph. I shall risk this conjecture: *Hitler wants to be defeated.* Hitler is blindly collaborating with the inevitable armies that will annihilate him, as the metal vultures and the dragon (which must have known that they were monsters) collaborated, mysteriously, with Hercules.

[1944]

On William Beckford's Vathek

Wilde attributes this joke to Carlyle: a biography of Michelangelo that would make no mention of the works of Michelangelo. So complex is reality, and so fragmentary and simplified is history, that an omniscient observer could write an indefinite, almost infinite, number of biographies of a man, each emphasizing different facts; we would have to read many of them before we realized that the protagonist was the same. Let us greatly simplify, and imagine that a life consists of 13,000 facts. One of the hypothetical biographies would record the series 11, 22, 33 . . .; another, the series 9, 13, 17, 21 . . .; another, the series 3, 12, 21, 30, 39. . . . A history of a man's dreams is not inconceivable; another, of all the organs of his body; another, of the mistakes he made; another, of all the moments when he thought about the Pyramids; another, of his dealings with the night and with the dawn. The above may seem merely fanciful, but unfortunately it is not. No one today resigns himself to writing the literary biography of an author or the military biography of a soldier; everyone prefers the genealogical biography, the economic biography, the psychiatric biography, the surgical biography, the typographical biography. One life of Poe consists of seven hundred octavo pages; the author, fascinated by changes of residence, barely manages one parenthesis for the Maelstrom or the cosmogony of 'Eureka.'

Another example: this curious revelation in the prologue to
a biography of Bolivar: 'As in the author's book on Napoleon, the battles are scarcely discussed.' Carlyle's joke pre-
dicted our contemporary literature: in 1943, the paradox
would be a biography of Michelangelo that allowed for
some mention of the works of Michelangelo.

The examination of a recent biography of William
Beckford (1760–1844) has provoked the above observations. William Beckford of Fonthill was the embodiment
of a rather trivial type of millionaire: distinguished gentleman, traveler, bibliophile, builder of palaces, and libertine. Chapman, his biographer, unravels (or tries to unravel)
his labyrinthine life, but omits an analysis of *Vathek*, the
novel whose final ten pages have brought William Beckford
his fame.

I have compared various critical works on *Vathek*. The
prologue that Mallarmé wrote for the 1876 edition abounds
in felicitous observations (for example: he points out that
the novel begins atop a tower from which the heavens
may be read in order to end in an enchanted subterranean vault), but it is written in an etymological dialect of
French that is difficult or impossible to read. Belloc (*A
Conversation with an Angel*, 1928), opines on Beckford
without condescending to explanations; he compares the
prose to that of Voltaire and judges him to be 'one of the
vilest men of his time.' Perhaps the most lucid evaluation
is that of Saintsbury in the eleventh volume of the *Cambridge History of English Literature*.

In essence, the fable of *Vathek* is not complex. Vathek
(Haroun Benalmotasim Vatiq Bila, the ninth Abbasid caliph) erects a Babylonian tower in order to decipher the

planets. They foretell a succession of wonders to be brought about by a man unlike any other who will come from an unknown land. A merchant arrives at the capital of the empire; his face is so atrocious that the guards who bring him before the caliph advance with eyes closed. The merchant sells a scimitar to the caliph, then disappears. Engraved on the blade are some mysterious changing characters which pique Vathek's curiosity. A man (who then also disappears) deciphers them; one day they mean, 'I am the least of the marvels in a place where everything is marvelous and worthy of the greatest Prince of the earth'; another day, 'Woe to the rash mortal who aspires to know that which he is not supposed to know.' The caliph surrenders to the magic arts; from the shadows, the voice of the merchant urges him to renounce the Muslim faith and worship the powers of darkness. If he will do that, the Palace of Subterranean Fire will be opened to him. Within its vaults he will be able to contemplate the treasures that the stars have promised him, the talismans that subdue the world, the diadems of the pre-Adamite sultans and of Suleiman Ben Daoud. The greedy caliph agrees; the merchant demands forty human sacrifices. Many bloody years pass; Vathek, his soul black from abominations, arrives at a deserted mountain. The earth opens; in terror and hope, Vathek descends to the bottom of the world. A pale and silent crowd of people who do not look at one another wanders through the magnificent galleries of an infinite palace. The merchant did not lie: the Palace of Subterranean Fire abounds in splendors and talismans, but it is also Hell. (In the congeneric story of Doctor Faustus, and in the many medieval legends that prefigured it,

Hell is the punishment for the sinner who makes a pact with the gods of Evil; here, it is both the punishment and the temptation.)

Saintsbury and Andrew Lang claim or suggest that the invention of the Palace of Subterranean Fire is Beckford's greatest achievement. I would maintain that it is the first truly atrocious Hell in literature.[1] I will venture this paradox: the most famous literary Avernus, the *dolente regno* of the *Divine Comedy*, is not an atrocious place; it is a place where atrocious things happen. The distinction is valid.

Stevenson ('A Chapter on Dreams') tells of being pursued in the dreams of his childhood by a certain abominable 'hue' of the color brown; Chesterton (*The Man Who Was Thursday*) imagines that at the western borders of the world there is perhaps a tree that is more or less than a tree; and that at the eastern borders, there is something, perhaps a tower, whose very shape is wicked. Poe, in his 'MS Found in a Bottle,' speaks of a southern sea where the ship itself will grow in bulk like the living body of the seaman; Melville devotes many pages of *Moby-Dick* to an elucidation of the horror of the unbearable whiteness of the whale. . . . I have given several examples, but perhaps it is enough to observe that Dante's Hell magnifies the notion of a jail; Beckford's, the tunnels of a nightmare. The *Divine Comedy* is the most justifiable and solid book in all literature, *Vathek* is a mere curiosity, 'the perfume and suppliance of a minute'; yet I believe that *Vathek* foretells, in however rudimentary a way, the satanic

1. In literature, that is, not in mysticism: the elective Hell of Swedenborg – *De coelo et inferno*, 545, 554 – is of an earlier date.

splendors of Thomas De Quincey and Poe, of Charles Baudelaire and Huysmans. There is an untranslatable English epithet, 'uncanny,' to denote supernatural horror; that epithet *(unheimlich* in German) is applicable to certain pages of *Vathek*, but not, as far as I recall, to any other book before it.

Chapman notes some of the books that influenced Beckford: the *Bibliothéque orientale* of Barthélemy d'Herbelot; Hamilton's *Quatre Facardins*; Voltaire's *La Princesse de Babylone*; the always reviled and admirable *Mille et une nuits* of Galland. To that list I would add Piranesi's *Carceri d'invenzione*: etchings, praised by Beckford, that depict mighty palaces which are also impenetrable labyrinths. Beckford, in the first chapter of *Vathek*, enumerates five palaces dedicated to the five senses; Marino, in the *Adone*, had already described five similar gardens.

William Beckford needed only three days and two nights in the winter of 1782 to write the tragic history of his caliph. He wrote it in French; Henley translated it into English in 1785. The original is unfaithful to the translation; Saintsbury observes that eighteenth-century French is less suitable than English for communicating the 'undefined horrors' (the phrase is Beckford's) of this unusual story.

Henley's English version is volume 856 of the Everyman's Library; Perrin, in Paris, has published the original text, revised and prologued by Mallarmé. It is strange that Chapman's laborious bibliography does not mention that revision and that prologue.

[1943]

An Overwhelming Film

Citizen Kane (called *The Citizen* in Argentina) has at least two plots. The first, pointlessly banal, attempts to milk applause from dimwits; a vain millionaire collects statues, gardens, palaces, swimming pools, diamonds, cars, libraries, men and women. Like an earlier collector (whose observations are usually ascribed to the Holy Ghost), he discovers that this cornucopia of miscellany is a vanity of vanities: all is vanity. At the point of death, he yearns for one single thing in the universe, the humble sled he played with as a child!

The second plot is far superior. It links the Koheleth to the memory of another nihilist, Franz Kafka. A kind of metaphysical detective story, its subject (both psychological and allegorical) is the investigation of a man's inner self, through the works he has wrought, the words he has spoken, the many lives he has ruined. The same technique was used by Joseph Conrad in *Chance* (1914) and in that beautiful film *The Power and the Glory*: a rhapsody of miscellaneous scenes without chronological order. Overwhelmingly, endlessly, Orson Welles shows fragments of the life of the man, Charles Foster Kane, and invites us to combine them and to reconstruct him. Forms of multiplicity and incongruity abound in the film: the first scenes record the treasures amassed by Kane; in one of the last, a poor woman, luxuriant and suffering, plays with an enormous jigsaw puzzle on the floor of a palace that is also a museum. At the end we realize that the fragments are not governed by any secret unity: the detested Charles Foster Kane is a simulacrum, a chaos of appearances. (A possible corollary, foreseen by David Hume, Ernst Mach, and our own Macedonio Fernández: no man knows who he is, no man is anyone.) In a story by Chesterton – 'The Head of Caesar,' I think – the hero observes that nothing is so frightening as a labyrinth with no center. This film is precisely that labyrinth.

We all know that a party, a palace, a great undertaking, a lunch for writers and journalists, an atmosphere of cordial and spontaneous camaraderie, are essentially horrendous. *Citizen Kane* is the first film to show such things with an awareness of this truth.

The production is, in general, worthy of its vast subject. The cinematography has a striking depth, and there are shots whose farthest planes (like Pre-Raphaelite paintings) are as precise and detailed as the close-ups.

I venture to guess, nonetheless, that *Citizen Kane* will endure as certain Griffith or Pudovkin films have 'endured' – films whose historical value is undeniable but which no one cares to see again. It is too gigantic, pedantic, tedious. It is not intelligent, though it is the work of genius – in the most nocturnal and Germanic sense of that bad word.

[1941]

Our Poor Individualism

There is no end to the illusions of patriotism. In the first century of our era Plutarch mocked those who declared that the Athenian moon is better than the Corinthian moon; Milton, in the seventeenth, observed that God is in the habit of revealing Himself first to His Englishmen; Fichte, at the beginning of the nineteenth, declared that to have character and to be German are obviously one and the same thing. Here in Argentina we are teeming with nationalists, driven, they claim, by the worthy or innocent resolve of promoting the best traits of the Argentine people. Yet they ignore the Argentine people; in their polemics they prefer to define them as a function of some external fact, the Spanish conquistadors, say, or an imaginary Catholic tradition, or 'Saxon imperialism.'

The Argentine, unlike the Americans of the North and almost all Europeans, does not identify with the State. This is attributable to the circumstance that the governments in this country tend to be awful, or to the general fact that the State is an inconceivable abstraction.[1] One thing is certain: the Argentine is an individual, not a citizen. Aphorisms such as Hegel's 'The state is the reality of the moral idea' strike him as sinister jokes. Films made

1. The State is impersonal; the Argentine can only conceive of personal relations. Therefore, to him, robbing public funds is not a crime. I am noting a fact; I am not justifying or excusing it.

in Hollywood often hold up for admiration the case of a man (usually a journalist) who seeks out the friendship of a criminal in order to hand him over to the police; the Argentine, for whom friendship is a passion and the police a mafia, feels that this 'hero' is an incomprehensible swine. He feels with Don Quixote that 'everybody hath sins of his own to answer for' and that 'it is not seemly, that honest men should be the executioners of their fellow-creatures, on account of matters with which they have no concern' (*Quixote* I, XXII). More than once, confronted with the vain symmetries of the Spanish style, I have suspected that we are irredeemably different from Spain; these two lines from the *Quixote* have sufficed to convince me of my error; they seem to be the secret, tranquil symbol of our affinity. This is profoundly confirmed by a single night in Argentine literature: the desperate night when a sergeant in the rural police shouted that he was not going to consent to the crime of killing a brave man, and started fighting against his own soldiers alongside the fugitive Martín Fierro.

The world, for the European, is a cosmos in which each individual personally corresponds to the role he plays; for the Argentine, it is a chaos. The European and the North American consider that a book that has been awarded any kind of prize must be good; the Argentine allows for the possibility that the book might not be bad, despite the prize. In general, the Argentine does not believe in circumstances. He may be unaware of the fable that humanity always includes thirty-six just men – the Lamed Wufniks – who are unknown to one another, but who secretly sustain the universe; if he hears of it, it does not strike him as strange that these worthies are obscure and anonymous. . . . His popular hero is the lone man who quarrels with the group, either actually (Fierro, Moreira, the Black Ant), potentially, or in the past (Segundo Sombra). Other literatures do not record analogous events. Consider, for example, two great European writers: Kipling and Franz Kafka. At first glance, the two have nothing in common, but Kipling's subject is the defense of order, of an order (the road in *Kim*, the bridge in *The Bridge-Builders*, the Roman wall in *Puck of Pook's Hill*); Kafka's, the unbearable, tragic solitude of the individual who lacks even the lowliest place in the order of the universe.

It may be said that the traits I have pointed out are merely negative or anarchic; it may be added that they are not subject to political explanation. I shall venture to suggest the opposite. The most urgent problem of our time (already denounced with prophetic lucidity by the near-forgotten Spencer) is the gradual interference of the State in the acts of the individual; in the battle with this evil, whose names are communism and Nazism, Argentine individualism, though perhaps useless or harmful until now, will find its justification and its duties.

Without hope and with nostalgia, I think of the abstract possibility of a party that had some affinity with the Argentine people; a party that would promise (let us say) a strict minimum of government.

Nationalism seeks to captivate us with the vision of an infinitely tiresome State; this utopia, once established on earth, would have the providential virtue of making everyone yearn for, and finally build, its antithesis.

[1946]

73

On Oscar Wilde

To speak Wilde's name is to speak of a dandy who was also a poet; it is to evoke the image of a gentleman dedicated to the meager proposition of shocking by means of cravats and metaphors. It is also to evoke the notion of art as an elite or occult game – as in the tapestries of Hugh Vereker or of Stefan George – and the poet as a laborious *'monstrorum artifex'* [maker of monsters] (Pliny, XXVIII). It is to evoke the tired crepuscule of the nineteenth century, with its oppressive pomp of hothouse and masked ball. None of these evocations is false, but all of them, I maintain, correspond to partial truths, and contradict or disregard well-known facts.

Let us consider, for example, the idea that Wilde was a kind of symbolist. A nebula of circumstances supports it: in 1881, Wilde was the leader of the aesthetes, and ten years later of the decadents; Rebecca West perfidiously accuses him (*Henry James*, III) of giving the second of these two sects 'the middle-class touch'; the vocabulary of the poem 'The Sphinx' is studiously magnificent; Wilde was a friend to Schwob and to Mallarmé. The notion is refuted, however, by an essential fact: in verse or in prose, Wilde's syntax is always very simple. Of the many British writers, none is so accessible to foreigners. Readers who are incapable of deciphering a single paragraph by Kipling or a stanza of William Morris begin reading *Lady Windermere's Fan* and finish it that same afternoon. Wilde's meter is spontaneous, or seeks to appear spontaneous; his complete work does not include a single experimental line such as this hard and wise Alexandrine by Lionel Johnson: 'Alone with Christ, desolate else, left by mankind.'

Wilde's *technical* insignificance may be an argument in favor of his intrinsic greatness. If Wilde's work corresponded to the nature of his fame, it would consist merely of artifices, after the fashion of *Les Palais nomades* or *Los crepúsculos del jardín*. In Wilde's work such artifices are numerous – we can mention the eleventh chapter of *Dorian Gray* or 'The Harlot's House' or 'Symphony in Yellow' – but their adjectival nature is obvious. Wilde can do without these 'purple patches' a phrase Ricketts and Hesketh Pearson credit him with coining, but which is already inscribed in the preamble to Cicero's *In Pisonem*. This misattribution is proof of the custom of linking the notion of decorative passages to Wilde's name.

Reading and rereading Wilde over the years, I note a fact that his panegyrists seem not even to have suspected: the elementary and demonstrable fact that Wilde is nearly always right. 'The Soul of Man under Socialism' is not only eloquent; it is correct. The miscellaneous notes he so copiously contributed to the *Pall Mall Gazette* and the *Speaker* abound in limpid observations that exceed the very best abilities of Leslie Stephen or Saintsbury. Wilde has been accused of practicing a kind of *ars combinatoria*, in the manner of Ramón Llull; this may be applicable to certain of his jokes ('One of those British faces which, once seen, are always forgotten') but not to the pronouncement that music reveals to us an unknown and perhaps real past ('The Critic as Artist'), or that all men kill the thing they love (*The Ballad of Reading Gaol*), or that to repent of an action is to modify the past (*De Profundis*), or that – and the statement is not unworthy of León Bloy or Swedenborg[1] – there is no man who is not, at each moment, all that he has been and will be (*De Profundis*). I do not transcribe these lines so that the reader may revere them; I produce them as signs of a mentality that differs greatly from the one generally attributed to Wilde. If I am not mistaken, he was much more than a sort of Irish Moréas; he was a man of the eighteenth century who occasionally condescended to the games of symbolism. Like Gibbon, like Johnson, like Voltaire, he was a wit; a wit who was also right. He existed 'in order, at last, to speak fateful words, in short, a classic.'[2] He gave the century what the century demanded – *comédies larmoyantes* for the majority and verbal arabesques for the few – and he accomplished these dissimilar things with a kind of negligent felicity. Perfection has injured him; his work is so harmonious that it can seem inevitable and even banal. It takes an effort for us to imagine the universe without Wilde's epigrams; that difficulty does not make them any less plausible.

1. Cf. the curious hypothesis of Leibniz, which so scandalized Arnauld: 'The concept of each individual encloses *a priori* all the events that will happen to him.' According to this dialectical fatalism, the fact that Alexander the Great would die in Babylon is one of the qualities of that king, like pride.

2. The phrase is from Reyes, who applies it to the Mexican man (*Reloj de sol*, 158).

A passing observation. The name of Oscar Wilde is linked to the cities of the plain; his glory, to condemnation and jail. Yet (and Hesketh Pearson has sensed this well), the fundamental flavor of his work is happiness. By contrast, the estimable work of Chesterton, that prototype of physical and moral health, is always on the point of becoming a nightmare. Horrors and things diabolical lurk within it; the most innocuous page can take on the forms of terror. Chesterton is a man who wishes to recover childhood; Wilde, a man who retains, despite the habits of wickedness and misfortune, an invulnerable innocence.

Like Chesterton, like Lang, like Boswell, Wilde is one of the fortunates who can forego the approval of critics and even, at times, of the reader, because the delight we derive from his company is constant and irresistible.

[1946]

The Wall and the Books

He, whose long wall the wand'ring Tartar bounds . . .

—*Dundad* III, 76

I read, a few days ago, that the man who ordered the building of the almost infinite Chinese Wall was that first Emperor, Shih Huang Ti, who also decreed the burning of all the books that had been written before his time. That these two vast undertakings – the five or six hundred leagues of stone against the barbarians, and the rigorous abolition of history, that is, of the past – were the work of the same person and were, in a sense, his attributes, inexplicably satisfied and, at the same time, disturbed me. To investigate the reasons for that emotion is the purpose of this note.

Historically, there is nothing mysterious about these two measures. At the time of the wars of Hannibal, Shih Huang Ti, king of Tsin, conquered the Six Kingdoms and put an end to the feudal system; he built the wall because walls were defenses; he burned the books because his opponents invoked them to praise earlier emperors. Burning books and erecting fortifications are the usual occupations of princes; the only thing unique about Shih Huang Ti was the scale on which he worked. That, at least, is the opinion of certain Sinologists, but I believe that both acts were something more than an exaggeration or hyperbole of trivial dispositions. To enclose an orchard or a garden is common, but not an empire. Nor is it a small matter to require the most traditional of races to renounce the memory of its past, mythical or real. Chinese chronology was already three thousand years long (and included the Yellow Emperor and Chuang Tzu and Confucius and Lao Tzu) when Shih Huang Ti ordered that history would begin with him.

Shih Huang Ti had exiled his mother as a libertine; the orthodox saw this stern justice as an impiety; Shih Huang Ti, perhaps, wanted to erase the canonical books because they condemned him; Shih Huang Ti, perhaps, wanted to abolish all the past to abolish a single memory: his mother's dishonor. (Not unlike a king, in Judea, who killed all the children in order to kill one child.) This speculation is tenable, but it tells us nothing about the wall, the other side of the myth. Shih Huang Ti, according to the historians, prohibited the mention of death and searched for the elixir of immortality and cloistered himself in a figurative palace with as many rooms as the days in the year; these facts suggest that the wall in space and the bonfire in time were magic barriers intended to stop death. All things desire to persist in their being, Baruch Spinoza wrote; perhaps the Emperor and his magicians believed that immortality was intrinsic and that decay could not enter a closed sphere. Perhaps the Emperor wanted to recreate the beginning of time and called himself the First to truly be the first, and called himself Huang Ti to somehow be Huang Ti, the legendary emperor who invented writing and the compass. It was he who, according to the *Book of Rites*, gave things their true names; similarly, Shih Huang Ti boasted, on inscriptions that still exist, that all things under his reign had the names that befitted them. He dreamed of founding an immortal dynasty; he decreed that his heirs should be called Second Emperor, Third Emperor, Fourth Emperor, and so on to infinity. . . . I have spoken of a magic plan; it may also be supposed that the building of the wall and the burning of the books were not simultaneous acts. Thus (depending on the order we choose) we would have the image of a king who began by destroying and then resigned himself to conserving; or the image of a disillusioned king who destroyed what he had once defended. Both conjectures are dramatic; but they lack, as far as I know, historical foundation. Herbert Allen Giles recounts that anyone who concealed books was branded with a hot iron and condemned to work on the endless wall until the day of his death. This favors or tolerates another interpretation. Perhaps the wall was a metaphor; perhaps Shih Huang Ti condemned those who adored the past to a work as vast as the past, as stupid and as useless. Perhaps the wall was a challenge and Shih Huang Ti thought, 'Men love the past and against that love there is nothing that I nor my executioners can do, but someday there will be a man who feels as I do, and he will destroy my wall, as I have destroyed the books, and he will erase my memory and will be my shadow and my mirror and will not know it.' Perhaps Shih Huang Ti walled his empire because he knew that it was fragile, and destroyed the books because he knew that they were sacred books,

books that teach what the whole universe teaches or the conscience of every man. Perhaps the burning of the libraries and the building of the wall are acts that in some secret way erase each other.

The unyielding wall which, at this moment and all moments, casts its system of shadows over lands I shall never see, is the shadow of a Caesar who ordered the most reverent of nations to burn its past; that idea is what moves us, quite apart from the speculations it allows. (Its virtue may be in the contrast between construction and destruction, on an enormous scale.) Generalizing, we might infer that *all* forms have virtue in themselves and not in an imagined 'content.' That would support the theory of Benedetto Croce; by 1877, Pater had already stated that all the arts aspire to resemble music, which is nothing but form. Music, states of happiness, mythology, faces worn by time, certain twilights and certain places, all want to tell us something, or have told us something we shouldn't have lost, or are about to tell us something; that imminence of a revelation as yet unproduced is, perhaps, the aesthetic fact.

[1950]

The Innocence of Layamon

Legouis saw the paradox of Layamon but not his pathos. The preamble to the *Brut*, written in the third person at the beginning of the thirteenth century, contains the facts of his life. Layamon writes:

There was in the land a priest named Layamon; he was the son of Leovenath (may God have mercy on his soul!), and he lived in Emley in a noble church on the banks of the Severn, a good place to be. It came to his mind the idea of relating the exploits of Englishmen, what they were named and where they came from, the earliest own-ers of our England, after the Great Flood. . . . Layamon traveled throughout the land and acquired the noble books that were his models. He took the English book made by St Bede; he took another in Latin made by St Albin and St Augustine, who brought us the faith; he took a third and placed it in the middle, the work of a French cleric named Wace, who knew how to write well, and gave it to the noble Leonor, queen of the great Henry. Layamon opened those three books and turned the pages; he looked at them lovingly – may God have mercy on him! – and picked up the pen and wrote on parchment and summoned the right words and made the three books into one. Now Layamon, for the love of God Omnipotent, begs those who read this book and learn

the truths it teaches to pray for the soul of his father, who
begot him, and for the soul of his mother, who bore him,
and for his own soul, to make it better. Amen.

Thirty thousand irregular verses then recount the battles
of the Britons, particularly Arthur, against the Picts, the
Norse, and the Saxons.

The first impression, and perhaps the last, given by
Layamon's preamble is of an infinite, almost incredible,
ingenuousness. Adding to this impression is the poet's
childlike trait of saying 'Layamon' for 'I,' but behind
the innocent words the emotion is complex. Layamon is
moved not only by the subject matter of the songs, but
also by the almost magical circumstance of seeing himself singing them; this reciprocity corresponds to the *'Illo
Virgilium me tempore'* [In that time, Virgil] of the *Georgics*
or to the beautiful *'Ego ille qui quondam'* [I, who one day]
that someone wrote to preface the *Aeneid*.

A legend recounted by Dionysius of Halicarnassus and
famously adopted by Virgil states that Rome was founded
by men descended from Aeneas, the Trojan who battles
Achilles in the pages of the *Iliad*; similarly a *Historia Regum
Britanniae* from the beginning of the twelfth century
attributes the founding of London ('Citie that some tyme
cleped was New Troy') to Aeneas' great-grandson Brutus,
whose name would be perpetuated in Britannia. Brutus is
the first king in Layamon's secular chronicle; he is followed by others who have known rather varied fortunes
in later literature: Hudibras, Lear, Gorboduc, Ferrex and
Porrex, Lud, Cymbeline, Vortigern, Uther Pendragon
(Uther Dragon's Head), and Arthur of the Round Table,

'the king who was and shall be,' according to his mysterious epitaph. Arthur is mortally wounded in his last battle, but Merlin – who in the *Brut* is not the son of the Devil but of a silent golden phantom loved by his mother in dreams – prophesies that he will return (like Barbarossa) when his people need him. Fruitlessly waging war against him are those rebellious hordes, the 'pagan dogs' of Hengest, the Saxons who were scattered over the face of England, beginning in the fifth century.

It has been said that Layamon was the first English poet; it is more accurate and more poignant to think of him as the last of the Saxon poets. The latter, converted to the faith of Jesus, applied the harsh accents and the military images of the Germanic epics to the new mythology (the Twelve Apostles, in one of Cynewulf's poems, are skilled in the use of shields and fend off a sudden attack by swordsmen; in the *Exodus*, the Israelites who cross the Red Sea are Vikings); Layamon applied the same rigor to the courtly and magical fictions of the *Matière de Bretagne*. Because of his subject matter, or a large part of it, he is one of the many poets of the Breton Cycle, a distant colleague of that anonymous writer who revealed to Francesca da Rimini and Paolo the love they felt for each other without knowing it. In spirit, he is a lineal descendant of those Saxon rhapsodists who reserved their joyful words for the description of battles and who, in four centuries, did not produce a single amatory stanza. Layamon has forgotten the metaphors of his ancestors – in the *Brut*, the sea is not the 'whale's path,' nor are arrows 'vipers of war' – but the vision of the world is the same. Like Stevenson, like Flaubert, like so many men of letters, the sedentary cleric takes pleasure in verbal violence; where Wace wrote, 'On that day the Britons killed Passent and the Irish King,' Layamon expands:

> And Uther the Good said these words: 'Passent, here you will remain, for here comes Uther on his horse!' He hit him on his head and knocked him down and plunged his sword down his throat (giving him a food that was new to him) and the point of the sword disappeared into the ground. Then Uther said: 'Now it is well with you, Irishman; all England is yours. I deliver it into your hands so that you may stay here and live with us. Look, here it is; now you will have it forever.'

In every line of Anglo-Saxon verse there are certain words, two in the first half and one in the second, that begin with the same consonant or vowel. Layamon tries to observe that old metrical law, but the octosyllabic couplets of Wace's *Geste des Bretons* – one of the three 'noble books' – continually distract him with the new temptation to rhyme, and so we have *brother* after *other* and *night* after *light*. . . . The Norman Conquest took place around the middle of the eleventh century; the *Brut* comes from the beginning of the thirteenth, but the vocabulary of the poem is almost entirely Germanic; in its thirty thousand lines there are not even fifty words of French origin. Here is a passage that scarcely prefigures the English language but has evident affinities with the German:

> And seothe ich cumen wulle
> to mine kineriche

and wumien mid Brutten
mid muchelere wunne.

Those were Arthur's last words. Their meaning is: 'And then I shall go to my kingdom, and I shall dwell among Britons with great delight.'

Layamon ardently sang of the ancient battles of the Britons against the Saxon invaders as if he himself were not a Saxon, and as if the Britons and the Saxons had not been, since that day in Hastings, conquered by the Normans. This fact is extraordinary and leads to various speculations. Layamon, son of Leovenath (Liefnoth), lived not far from Wales, the bulwark of the Celts and the source (according to Gaston Paris) of the complex myth of Arthur; his mother might well have been a Briton. This theory is possible, unverifiable, and impoverished; one could also suppose that the poet was the son and grandson of Saxons, but that, at heart, the *jus soli* was stronger than the *jus sanguinis*. This is not very different from the Argentine with no Querandí blood who identifies with the Indian defenders of his land rather than with the Spaniards of Cabrera or Juan de Garay. Another possibility is that Layamon, whether knowingly or not, gave the Britons of the *Brut* the value of Saxons, and the Saxons the value of Normans. The riddles, the Bestiary, and Cynewulf's curious runes prove that such cryptographic or allegorical exercises were not alien to that ancient literature; something, however, tells me that this speculation is fantastic. If Layamon had thought that yesterday's conquerors were the conquered of today, and today's conquerors could be the conquered of tomorrow, he would, I think, have used the simile of the Wheel of Fortune, which is in the *De Consolatione*, or had recourse to the prophetic books of the Bible, not to the intricate romance of Arthur.

The subjects of the earlier epics were the exploits of a hero or the loyalty that warriors owe to their captain; the true subject of the *Brut* is England. Layamon could not foresee that two centuries after his death his alliteration would be ridiculous ('I can not geste – rum, ram, ruf – by lettre,' says a character in Chaucer) and his language, a rustic jargon. He could not have suspected that his insults to the Hengests' Saxons would be the last words in the Saxon language, destined to die and be born again in the English language. According to the Germanic scholar Ker, he barely knew the literature whose tradition he inherited; he knew nothing of the wanderings of Widsith among the Persians and Hebrews or of Beowulf's battle at the bottom of the red marsh. He knew nothing of the great verses from which his own were to spring; perhaps he would not have understood them. His curious isolation, his solitude, make him, now, touching. 'No one knows who he himself is,' said León Bloy; of that personal ignorance there is no symbol better than this forgotten man, who abhorred his Saxon heritage with Saxon vigor, and who was the last Saxon poet and never knew it.

[1951]

Coleridge's Dream

The lyric fragment 'Kubla Khan' (fifty-odd rhymed and irregular lines of exquisite prosody) was dreamed by the English poet Samuel Taylor Coleridge on a summer day in 1797. Coleridge writes that he had retired to a farm near Exmoor; an indisposition obliged him to take a sedative; sleep overcame him a few moments after reading a passage in Purchas that describes the construction of a palace by Kublai Khan, the emperor whose fame in the West was the work of Marco Polo. In Coleridge's dream, the text he had coincidentally read sprouted and grew; the sleeping man intuited a series of visual images and, simply, the words that expressed them. After a few hours he awoke, certain that he had composed, or received, a poem of some three hundred lines. He remembered them with particular clarity and was able to transcribe the fragment that is now part of his work. An unexpected visitor interrupted him, and it was later impossible for him to recall the rest. 'To his no small surprise and mortification,' Coleridge wrote, 'that though he still retained some vague and dim recollection of the general purport of the vision, yet, with the exception of some eight or ten scattered lines and images, all the rest had passed away like the images on the surface of a stream into which a stone has been cast, but, alas! without the after restoration of the latter!' Swinburne felt that what he had been able to recover was the supreme example of music in the English language, and that the person capable of analyzing it would be able – the metaphor is Keats' – to unravel a rainbow. Translations or summaries of poems whose principal virtue is music are useless and may be harmful; it is best simply to bear in mind, for now, that Coleridge was given a page of undisputed splendor *in a dream*.

The case, although extraordinary, is not unique. In his psychological study, *The World of Dreams*, Havelock Ellis has compared it with that of the violinist and composer Giuseppe Tartini, who dreamed that the Devil (his slave) was playing a marvelous sonata on the violin; when he awoke, the dreamer deduced, from his imperfect memory, the '*Trillo del Diavolo*.' Another classic example of unconscious cerebration is that of Robert Louis Stevenson, to whom – as he himself described it in his 'Chapter on Dreams' – one dream gave the plot of *Olalla* and another, in 1884, the plot of *Jekyll and Hyde*. Tartini, waking, wanted to imitate the music he had heard in a dream; Stevenson received outlines of stories – forms in general – in his. Closer to Coleridge's verbal inspiration is the one attributed by the Venerable Bede to Caedmon (*Historia ecclesiastica gentis Anglorum* IV, 24). The case occurred at the end of the seventh century in the missionary and warring England of the Saxon kingdoms. Caedmon was an uneducated shepherd and was no longer young; one night he slipped away from some festivity because he knew that the harp would be passed to him and he didn't know how to sing. He fell asleep in a stable, among the horses, and in a dream someone called him by his name and ordered him to sing. Caedmon replied that he did not know how, but the voice said, 'Sing about the origin of created things.' Then Caedmon recited verses he had never heard. He did not forget them when he awoke, and was able to repeat them to the monks at the nearby monastery of Hild. Although he couldn't read, the monks explained passages of sacred history to him and he,

> as it were, chewing the cud, converted the same into most harmonious verse; and sweetly repeating the same made his masters in their turn his hearers. He sang the creation of the world, the origin of man, and all the history of Genesis: and made many verses on the departure of the children of Israel out of Egypt, and their entering into the land of promise, with many other histories from holy writ; the incarnation, passion, resurrection of our Lord, and his ascension into heaven; the coming of the Holy Ghost, and the preaching of the apostles; also the terror of future judgment, the horror of the pains of hell, and the delights of heaven; besides many more about the Divine benefits and judgments . . .

He was the first sacred poet of the English nation. 'None could ever compare with him,' Bede wrote, 'for he did not learn the art of poetry from men, but from God.' Years later, he foretold the hour of his death and awaited it in sleep. Let us hope that he met his angel again.

At first glance, Coleridge's dream may seem less astonishing than that of his precursor. 'Kubla Khan' is a remarkable composition, and the nine-line hymn dreamed by Caedmon barely displays any virtues beyond its oneiric

origin; but Coleridge was already a poet while Caedmon's vocation was revealed to him. There is, however, a
later event, which turns the marvel of the dream that
engendered 'Kubla Khan' into something nearly unfath-
omable. If it is true, the story of Coleridge's dream began
many centuries before Coleridge and has not yet ended.

The poet's dream occurred in 1797 (some say 1798),
and he published his account of the dream in 1816 as a
gloss or justification of the unfinished poem. Twenty
years later, in Paris, the first Western version of one of
those universal histories that are so abundant in Persian
literature appeared in fragmentary form: the *Compen-
dium of Histories* by Rashid al-Din, which dates from the
fourteenth century. One line reads as follows: 'East of
Shang-tu, Kublai Khan built a palace according to a plan
that he had seen in a dream and retained in his memory.'
The one who wrote this was a vizier of Ghazan Mah-
mud, a descendant of Kublai.

A Mongolian emperor, in the thirteenth century, dreams
a palace and builds it according to his vision; in the eighteenth century, an English poet, who could not have known
that this construction was derived from a dream, dreams a
poem about the palace. Compared with this symmetry of
souls of sleeping men who span continents and centuries,
the levitations, resurrections, and apparitions in the sacred
books seem to me quite little, or nothing at all.

How is it to be explained? Those who automatically
reject the supernatural (I try always to belong to this
group) will claim that the story of the two dreams is a
coincidence, a line drawn by chance, like the shapes of
lions or horses that are sometimes formed by clouds.

Others will argue that the poet somehow knew that the Emperor had dreamed the palace, and then claimed he had dreamed the poem in order to create a splendid fiction that would palliate or justify the truncated and rhapsodic quality of the verses.[1] This seems reasonable, but it forces us to arbitrarily postulate a text unknown to Sinologists in which Coleridge was able to read, before 1816, about Kublai's dream.[2] More appealing are the hypotheses that transcend reason: for example, that after the palace was destroyed, the soul of the Emperor penetrated Coleridge's soul in order that the poet could rebuild it in words, which are more lasting than metal and marble.

The first dream added a palace to reality; the second, which occurred five centuries later, a poem (or the beginning of a poem) suggested by the palace; the similarity of the dreams hints of a plan; the enormous length of time involved reveals a superhuman executor. To speculate on the intentions of that immortal or long-lived being would be as foolish as it is fruitless, but it is legitimate to suspect that he has not yet achieved his goal. In 1691, Father Gerbillon of the Society of Jesus confirmed that ruins were all that was left of Kublai Khan's palace; of the poem, we know that barely fifty lines were salvaged. Such facts raise the possibility that this series of dreams and works has

1. At the end of the 18th or beginning of the 19th century, judged by readers with classical taste, 'Kubla Khan' was much more scandalous than it is now. In 1884, Coleridge's first biographer, Traill, could still write: 'The extravagant dream poem 'Kubla Khan' is little more than a psychological curiosity.'

2. See John Livingston Lowes, *The Road to Xanadu* (1927) 358, 585.

not yet ended. The first dreamer was given the vision of the palace, and he built it; the second, who did not know of the other's dream, was given the poem about the palace. If this plan does not fail, someone, on a night centuries removed from us, will dream the same dream, and not suspect that others have dreamed it, and he will give it a form of marble or of music. Perhaps this series of dreams has no end, or perhaps the last one will be the key.

After writing this, I glimpsed or thought I glimpsed another explanation. Perhaps an archetype not yet revealed to mankind, an eternal object (to use Whitehead's term), is gradually entering the world; its first manifestation was the palace; its second, the poem. Whoever compares them will see that they are essentially the same.

[1951]

The Enigma of Shakespeare

The two final chapters of Paul Groussac's *Crítica literaria* are dedicated to the Shakespeare question, or as I have preferred to call it here, the enigma of Shakespeare. As you will have guessed, this is the theory that the individual William Shakespeare, who died in 1616, was not the father of the tragedies, comedies, history plays, and poems that are now admired throughout the world. In his two articles, Groussac defends the classic opinion, the opinion shared by all until the middle years of the nineteenth century, when Miss Delia Bacon, in a book with a prologue by Hawthorne – to a book Hawthorne had not read – elected to attribute the paternity of those works to the statesman and philosopher Francis Bacon, the founder and, in some sense, the martyr of modern science.

I, of course, believe that the William Shakespeare honored today in East and West was the author of the works we attribute to him, but I would like to add a few points to Groussac's argument. Moreover, in recent years a second candidacy has emerged, the most interesting of all from a psychological and, we might say, from a police detective point of view: that of the poet Christopher Marlowe, murdered in a tavern in Deptford, near London, in the year 1593.

Let us examine, first of all, the arguments against Shakespeare's paternity. They may be summarized as

follows: Shakespeare received a fairly rudimentary educa-
tion in the grammar school of his hometown, Stratford.
Shakespeare, as attested by his friend and rival, the dramatic poet Ben Jonson, possessed 'small Latin and less
Greek.' There are those who, in the nineteenth century,
discovered or believed they had discovered an encyclopedic erudition in Shakespeare's work. It seems to me that
while it is a fact that Shakespeare's vocabulary is gigantic,
even within the gigantic English language, it is one thing
to use terms from many disciplines and sciences and
another thing altogether to have a profound or even super-
ficial knowledge of those same disciplines and sciences.
We can recall the analogous case of Cervantes. I believe a
Mr Barby, in the nineteenth century, published a book entitled *Cervantes, Expert in Geography*.

The truth is that the aesthetic is inaccessible to many
people and they prefer to seek out the virtue of men of
genius – which Cervantes and Shakespeare indisputably
were – elsewhere: in their knowledge, for example. Miss
Delia Bacon and the rest claimed that the profession of
playwright was an insignificant one in the era of Eliza-
beth, the Virgin Queen, and James I, and that the erudition they believed they discovered in Shakespeare's work
could not have belonged to poor William Shakespeare,
for the author of those works had to be an encyclopedic
man. Miss Delia Bacon discovered that man in her homo-
nym, Francis Bacon.

The argument is as follows: Bacon was a man of vast
political and scientific ambitions; Bacon wanted to renew
science, to found what he called the *regnum hominis* or
kingdom of man. It would have been out of keeping

with his dignity as a statesman and philosopher to compose dramatic works. He therefore sought out the actor and theatrical impresario, William Shakespeare, to use his name as a pseudonym.

Those who endeavored to enrich Miss Bacon's thesis, or to carry it to an absurd extreme, had recourse – and now we are in the realm of the detective story, in the 'Gold Bug' of the future Edgar Allan Poe – to cryptography. Incredible as it may seem, they pored over the complete works of William Shakespeare in search of a line that begins with a B, followed by a line beginning with an A, then by one beginning with a C, the penultimate with an O, and the last with an N. In other words, they were seeking a secret signature by Bacon in his work. They did not find it. Then one of them, even more absurd than his predecessors, which seems difficult, remembered that the English word 'bacon' refers to the meat of the pig, and that Bacon, instead of signing his own name, even cryptographically or acrostically, might have preferred to sign 'hog' or 'pig' or 'swine' – an extraordinarily improbable thing, since no one makes that kind of joke with his own name. This particular individual, I believe, had the good fortune to run across a line that began with a P, followed by one that began not with an I but with a Y, and a third beginning with a G. He believed his strange hypothesis was amply justified by this lone pig discovered in the works of Shakespeare.

There is also a long, meaningless Latinate word in which some have discovered the anagram *'Francis Bacon sic scriptit'* or *'Francis Bacon fecit'* or something like that. One of the partisans of the Baconian thesis was Mark

Twain, who summarized all the arguments very wittily in a book entitled *Is Shakespeare Dead?*, which I recommend not for your convictions but for your amusement. All of this, as you can see, is purely speculative and hypothetical, and all of it was magisterially refuted by Groussac.

To those arguments, I would add others of diverse natures. Groussac speaks of the poor quality of the verse that has been attributed to Bacon; I would add that the minds of the two men are essentially and irreparably different. Bacon, of course, had a more modern mind than Shakespeare: Bacon had a sense of history; he felt that his era, the seventeenth century, was the beginning of a scientific age, and he wanted the veneration of the texts of Aristotle to be replaced by a direct investigation of nature.

Bacon was a precursor of what today we call science fiction; in his *New Atlantis*, he narrates the adventure of some travelers who arrive at a lost island in the Pacific on which many of the marvels of contemporary science have become realities. For example: there are ships that travel beneath the water, others that journey through the air; there are chambers in which rain, snow, storms, echoes, and rainbows are artificially created; there are fantastical zoos that exhaust the variety of all hybrids and current species of plants and animals.

Bacon's mind had no less of a propensity for metaphor than Shakespeare's, and here was a point of contact between the two, except that the metaphors differ greatly. Let us take, for example, a book of logic, such as John Stuart Mill's *System of Logic*, in which he points out the errors to which the human mind is prone. Mill, as many others have done, creates a classification of fallacies. Bacon, in doing the same thing, said that the human mind is not a perfectly flat mirror but a slightly concave or convex mirror, which distorts reality. He claimed that man is prone to error, and he called the errors to which we are prone 'idols,' and proceeded to list them.

First were the *'idola tribus,'* the idols of the tribe, the idols common to the entire human race. He declared that there are minds that note the affinities between things, and other minds that tend to notice or exaggerate the differences, and that the scientific observer must observe himself and correct this inclination to note differences or resemblances (differences or sympathies, Alfonso Reyes would say). Next, Bacon speaks of the idols of the cave, *'idola specus.'* In other words, each man, without knowing it, is prone to a certain type of error. Let us imagine a man, an intelligent man, to whom, say, the poetry of Heine, the philosophy of Spinoza, and the doctrines of Einstein or Freud are explained. If this man is anti-Semitic, he will tend to reject these works, simply because they are by Jews; if he is Jewish or philo-Semitic he will tend to accept them, simply because he feels sympathy for Jews. In both cases he will not impartially examine these works, but will subordinate his estimation of them to his likes or dislikes.

Next, Bacon speaks of the *'idola forum,'* the idols of the forum or marketplace; that is, the errors caused by language. He observes that language is the work not of philosophers but of the people. Chesterton would later maintain that language was invented by hunters, fishermen, and nomads and therefore is essentially poetic. In other words, language was not created to be a description of truth, it was created by arbitrary and fanciful people; language is continually leading us into error. If you say that someone is deaf, for example, and someone else doubts your word, you will say 'Yes, he's deaf as a post,' simply because you have at hand the convenient phrase, 'deaf as a post.'

To these idols, Bacon adds a fourth type, the *'idola teatri,'* idols of the theater. Bacon notes that all scientific systems – without excluding his own system of philosophy, observation, and induction; of going not from the general to the particular, but from the particular to the general – replace the real world with a world that is more or less fantastical, or, in any case, simplified. Thus we have Marxism, which examines all historic events by economic criteria; or we have a historian like Bossuet, who sees the hand of Providence in the entire historic process; or the theories of Spengler; or the contemporary doctrines of Toynbee; and none of them, Bacon would say, is reality, but is a theater, a representation of reality.

Furthermore, Bacon had no faith in the English language. He believed the vernacular languages had no power, and therefore had all his works translated into Latin. Bacon, archenemy of the Middle Ages, believed, like the Middle Ages, that there is a single international language: Latin.

Shakespeare, on the contrary, had, as we know, a profound feeling for the English language, which is perhaps unique among Western languages in its possession of what might be called a double register. For common words, for the ideas, say, of a child, a rustic, a sailor, or a peasant, it has words of Saxon origin, and for intellectual matters it has words derived from Latin. These words are never precisely synonymous, there is always a nuance of differentiation: it is one thing to say, Saxonly, 'dark' and another to say 'obscure'; one thing to say 'brotherhood' and another to say 'fraternity'; one thing – especially for poetry, which depends not only on atmosphere and on meaning but on the connotations of the atmosphere of words – to say, Latinly, 'unique' and another to say 'single.'

Shakespeare felt all this; one might say that a good part of Shakespeare's charm depends on this reciprocal play of Latin and Germanic terms. For example, when Macbeth, gazing at his own bloody hand, thinks it could stain the vast seas with scarlet, making of their green a single red thing, he says:

> Will all great Neptune's ocean wash this blood
> Clean from my hand? No, this my hand will rather
> The multitudinous seas incarnadine,
> Making the green one red.

In the third line we have long, sonorous, erudite Latin words: 'multitudinous,' 'incarnadine'; then, in the next, short Saxon words: 'green one red.'

There is, it seems to me, a psychological incompatibility between the minds of Bacon and Shakespeare, and this suffices to invalidate all of the Baconians' arguments and cryptographies, all the real or imaginary secret signatures they have discovered or think they have discovered in Shakespeare's work.

There are other candidates whom I choose to overlook, until I reach the least implausible of them all: the poet Christopher Marlowe, who is believed to have been murdered in the year 1593 at the age of twenty-nine, the age at which Keats died, the age at which Evaristo Carriego, our poet of the city's outskirts, died. Let us look briefly at Marlowe's life and work.

Marlowe was a 'university wit,' that is, he belonged to a group of young university students who condescended to the theater; moreover, Marlowe perfected the 'blank verse' that would become Shakespeare's instrument of choice, and in Marlowe's work there are lines no less splendid than those in Shakespeare. For example, the line so greatly admired by Unamuno that he said this single line was superior to all of Goethe's *Faust* – perhaps forgetting that perfection is easier in a single line than in a vast work, where it may be impossible. Marlowe's *Doctor Faustus*, like Goethe's *Faust*, finds himself before the specter of Helen (the idea that Helen of Troy was a ghost or apparition is already present in the ancients) and says to her, 'Sweet Helen, make me immortal with a kiss.' And then, 'O thou art fairer than the evening air clad in the beauty of a thousand stars.' He does not say 'evening sky,' but 'evening air.' All of Copernican space is present in that word *air*, the infinite space that was one of the revelations of the Renaissance, the space in which we still believe, despite Einstein, the space that came to supplant the Ptolomaic system which presides over Dante's triple comedy.

But let us return to Marlowe's tragic fate. In the final decades of the sixteenth century, there were fears in

England of a Catholic insurrection, incited by the power of Spain. At the same time, the city of London was agitated by riots. Many Flemish and French artisans had arrived in London and were being accused of eating 'the bread of fatherless children.' There was a kind of nationalist movement that attacked these foreigners and even threatened a general massacre. At that time, the State already had what we would call today a 'secret service,' and Marlowe was one of its men. It persecuted Catholics as well as Puritans; a playwright, Thomas Kyd, was arrested, and in his house certain papers were found. Among those papers was a manuscript with twenty or so heretical theses, some of them scandalous; one, for example, held that Jesus was a homosexual – there was, in addition, a defense of homosexuality – and another denied that a man, Christ, could be both man and God. There was also a panegyric to tobacco, which Ralegh had brought from America. Marlowe was part of the circle that surrounded Ralegh, the corsaire, the historian, who would later be executed, and in whose house were held the gatherings ominously called the School of Night.

Marlowe's characters, the characters with whom it is clear the author is in sympathy, are magnifications of Marlowe. They are atheists: Tamburlaine burns the Koran and finally, having conquered the world, wants, like Alexander, to conquer the heavens, and orders that his artillery be turned against the sky, and that black banners be hung from the sky to signify the hecatomb, the massacre of the gods: 'And set black streamers in the firmament,' etc. There is Doctor Faustus, who represents the Renaissance appetite to know everything, to read the book of nature, not in search of moral teachings, as in the Middle Ages, when the physiologies or bestiaries were compiled, but in search of the letters that compose the universe. There is *The Jew of Malta*, which is a magnification of greed.

Kyd's manuscript was examined by the police. He was tortured – torture is not an invention of our own time – and he confessed or declared, which was very natural, since his life was at stake, that this manuscript was not his but was written by the hand of Marlowe, with whom he had shared a room when the two of them worked together revising and correcting plays. A tribunal called the 'Star Chamber' judged this type of crime; Marlowe was told that in one week he would have to appear before this tribunal to be accused of blasphemy and atheism, and to defend himself. Then, two days before the hearing, Marlowe's murdered body was found in a tavern in Deptford.

It seems that four men, all belonging to the secret service, went to the tavern, had lunch, took a nap, went out for a stroll in the small country garden around the tavern, played chess or backgammon, I don't know which, and then had an argument about the bill. Marlowe took out his knife (knives were then the weapon of choice), and was supposedly stabbed in the eye with it, with his own knife, and died. Now, according to Calvin Hoffman's hypothesis, the man who died was not Marlowe but another man, any one of the other three. In that day and age, there was no way of identifying people, fingerprints were unknown, it was very easy to pass one man off as another, and Marlowe had told his friends of his intention of fleeing to Scotland, then an independent kingdom. Hoffmann's theory has it that Marlowe passed the dead man off as himself, then fled to Scotland, and from there sent his friend, the actor and theatrical impresario William Shakespeare, the works today attributed to Shakespeare. From Scotland, he had the manuscripts of *Macbeth, Hamlet, Othello, Anthony and Cleopatra,* etc., delivered to Shakespeare. Then Marlowe died, according to this theory, about four or five years before Shakespeare's death. The latter, after selling his theater and retiring to his hometown of Stratford, forgot all about his literary work and devoted himself to being the richest man in town, giving himself over to the pleasures of litigation against his neighbors until the death that befell him after a drinking bout with some actors who came from London to see him in the year 1616.

The argument I will sketch out against this hypothesis is that although Marlowe was a great poet and has lines not unworthy of Shakespeare – and there are, as well, many lines by Marlowe interspersed, as though lost, in the works of Shakespeare – there exists, nevertheless, an essential difference between the two. Coleridge used Spinoza's vocabulary in praise of Shakespeare. He said that Shakespeare was what Spinoza calls 'natura naturans,' creative nature: the force that takes all forms, that lies as if dead in rocks, that sleeps in plants, that dreams in the lives of animals, which are conscious only of the present moment, and that reaches its consciousness, or a certain consciousness in us, in mankind, the 'natura naturata.'

Hazlitt said that all the people who have existed in the universe are in Shakespeare; that is, Shakespeare had the power to multiply himself marvelously; to think of Shakespeare is to think of a crowd. However, in Marlowe's work we always have a central figure: the conqueror, Tamburlaine; the greedy man, Barabas; the man of science, Faust. The other characters are mere extras, they barely exist, whereas in Shakespeare's work all the characters exist, even incidental characters. The apothecary, for example, who sells poison to Romeo and says, 'My poverty, but not my will consents,' has already defined himself as a man by this single phrase. This appears to exceed Marlowe's possibilities.

In a letter to Frank Harris, Bernard Shaw wrote, 'Like Shakespeare I understand everything and everybody; and like Shakespeare I am nobody and nothing.' And here we arrive at the true enigma of Shakespeare: for us, he is one of the most visible men in the world, but he was certainly not that for his contemporaries. Here, the case of Cervantes is repeated. Lope de Vega wrote, 'No one is so stupid as to admire Miguel de Cervantes.' Gracián, in his *Agudeza y arte de ingenio* [Wit and the Art of Genius] does not find a single ingenious feature of the *Quixote* worth citing; Quevedo, in a romance, alludes offhandedly to Don Quixote's leanness. That is, Cervantes was almost invisible to his contemporaries; even his military action in the battle of Lepanto was so thoroughly forgotten that he himself had to remind people that he owed the loss of his arm to that battle.

As for Shakespeare, outside of an ambiguous accolade that speaks of his 'sugar sonnets,' his contemporaries do not seem to have had him much in view. The explanation for this, it seems to me, is that Shakespeare dedicated himself primarily to the genre of drama, except for the sonnets and the occasional poem such as 'The Phoenix and the Turtle' or 'The Passionate Pilgrim.' Every era believes that there is a literary genre that has a kind of primacy. Today, for example, any writer who has not written a novel is asked when he is going to write one. (I myself am continually being asked.) In Shakespeare's time, the literary work *par excellence* was the vast epic poem, and that idea persisted into the eighteenth century, when we have the example of Voltaire, the least epic of men, who nevertheless writes an epic because without an epic he would not have been a true man of letters for his contemporaries.

As for our own time, consider the cinema. When we think of the cinema, most of us think of actors or actresses; I think, anachronistically, of Miriam Hopkins and Katharine Hepburn – you can undoubtedly fill in more current names – or we think of directors: I think of Josef von Sternberg, who seems to me to be the greatest of all film directors, or, more recently, of Orson Welles or Hitchcock; you can insert whatever names you like. But we do not think of the screenwriter. I remember the films *The Dragnet, Underworld, Specter of the Rose* – that last title from Sir Thomas Browne – but Ben Hecht had to die a few days ago in order for me to remember that he was the author of the screenplays of these films that I have so often watched and praised.

Something analogous happened with plays in Shakespeare's time. Plays belonged to the acting company, not to their authors. Each time they were staged, new scenes with up-to-date touches were added. People laughed at Ben Jonson when he published his plays in all solemnity and gave them the title *Works*. 'What kind of "works" are these?' they said. 'These are just tragedies and comedies.' 'Works' would have to be lyric or epic or elegiac poems, for example, but not plays. So it is natural that his contemporaries did not admire Shakespeare. He wrote for actors.

One more mystery remains. Why does Shakespeare sell his theater, retire to his native town, and forget the works that are now one of the glories of humanity? An explanation has been formulated by the great writer De Quincey: it is that, for Shakespeare, publication was not the printed word. Shakespeare did not write to be read, but to be performed. The plays continued to be staged, and that was enough. Another explanation, this one psychological, is that Shakespeare needed the immediate stimulus of the theater. That is, when he wrote *Hamlet* or *Macbeth*, he adapted his words to one actor or another; as someone once said, when a character sings in Shakespeare's work it is because a certain actor knew how to play the lute or had a nice voice. Shakespeare needed this circumstantial stimulus. Goethe would say much later that all poetry is '*Gelegenheitsdichtung*,' poetry of circumstances. And Shakespeare, no longer driven by the actors or by the demands of the stage, felt no need to write. This, to my mind, is the most probable explanation. Groussac says that there are many writers who have made a display of their disdain for literary art, who have extended the line 'vanity of vanities, all is vanity' to literature; many literary people have disbelieved in literature. But, he says, all of them have given expression to their disdain, and all of those expressions are inexpressive if we compare them to Shakespeare's silence. Shakespeare, lord of all words, who arrives at the conviction that litera-ture is insignificant, and does not even seek the words to express that conviction; this is almost superhuman.

I said earlier that Bacon had a vivid sense of history. For Shakespeare, on the contrary, all characters, whether they are Danish, like Hamlet, Scottish, like Macbeth, Greek, Roman, or Italian, all the characters in all the many works, are treated as if they were Shakespeare's contemporaries. Shakespeare felt the variety of men, but not the variety of historical eras. History did not exist for him; it did exist for Bacon.

What was Shakespeare's philosophy? Bernard Shaw has tried to find it in the maxims so widely dispersed throughout his work that say life is essentially oneiric, illusory: 'We are such stuff as dreams are made of'; or when he says that life 'is a tale / Told by an idiot, full of sound and fury / Signifying nothing' or before that when he compares every man to an actor, which is a double play on words, because the king who speaks these words, Macbeth, is also an actor, a poor actor, 'that struts and frets his hour upon the stage / And then is heard no more.' But we may also believe that this does not correspond to any conviction of Shakespeare's, but only to what his characters might have felt at that moment. In other words, life may not be a nightmare, a senseless nightmare, for Shakespeare, but life may have been felt to be a nightmare by Macbeth, when he saw that the fates and the witches had deceived him.

Here we arrive at the central enigma of Shakespeare, which is perhaps the enigma of all literary creation. I return to Bernard Shaw, who was asked if he truly believed that the Holy Spirit had written the Bible, and who answered that the Holy Spirit had written not only the Bible, but all the books in the world. We no longer speak of the Holy Spirit; we now have another mythology; we say that a writer writes with his subconscious mind, or with the collective unconscious. Homer and Milton preferred to believe in the Muse: 'Sing, oh Muse, the wrath of Achilles,' said Homer, or the poets who were called Homer. All of them believed in a force of which they were the amanuenses. Milton refers directly to the Holy Spirit, whose temple is the bosom of the just. All of them felt that there is something more in a work than the voluntary intentions of its author. On the final page of the *Quixote*, Cervantes says that his intention has been nothing other than to mock books of chivalry. We can interpret this in two ways: we can suppose that Cervantes said this to make us understand that he had something else in mind, but we can also take these words literally, and think that Cervantes had no other aim – that Cervantes, without knowing it, created a work that mankind will not forget. He did so because he wrote the *Quixote* with the whole of his being, unlike the *Persiles*, for example, which he wrote with merely literary aims, and into which he did not put all that was dark and secret within him. Shakespeare may also have been assisted by distraction; it may help to be a little distracted in order to write a masterpiece. It may be that the intention of writing a masterpiece inhibits the writer, makes him keep a close watch on himself. It may be that aesthetic creation should be more like a dream, a dream unchecked by our attention. And this may have happened in Shakespeare's case.

Furthermore, Shakespeare's work has been progressively enriched by the generations of its readers. Undoubtedly Coleridge, Hazlitt, Goethe, Heine, Bradley, and Hugo have all enriched Shakespeare's work, and it will undoubtedly be read in another way by readers to come. Perhaps this is one possible definition of the work of genius: a book of genius is a book that can be read in a slightly or very different way by each generation. This is what happened with the Bible. Someone has compared the Bible to a musical instrument that has been tuned infinitely. We can read Shakespeare's work, but we do not know how it will be read in a century, or in ten centuries, or even, if universal history continues, in a hundred centuries. We do know that for us the work of Shakespeare is virtually infinite, and the enigma of Shakespeare is only one part of that other enigma, artistic creation, which, in turn, is only a facet of another enigma: the universe.

[1964]

Blindness

In the course of the many lectures – too many lectures – I have given, I've observed that people tend to prefer the personal to the general, the concrete to the abstract. I will begin, then, by referring to my own modest blindness. Modest, because it is total blindness in one eye, but only partial in the other. I can still make out certain colors; I can still see blue and green. And yellow, in particular, has remained faithful to me. I remember when I was young I used to linger in front of certain cages in the Palermo zoo: the cages of the tigers and leopards. I lingered before the tigers' gold and black. Yellow is still with me, even now. I have written a poem, entitled 'The Gold of the Tigers,' in which I refer to this friendship.

People generally imagine the blind as enclosed in a black world. There is, for example, Shakespeare's line: 'Looking on darkness which the blind do see.' If we understand 'darkness' as 'blackness,' then Shakespeare is wrong.

One of the colors that the blind – or at least this blind man – do not see is black; another is red. *Le rouge et le noir* are the colors denied us. I, who was accustomed to sleeping in total darkness, was bothered for a long time at having to sleep in this world of mist, in the greenish or bluish mist, vaguely luminous, which is the world of the blind. I wanted to lie down in darkness. The world of the blind is not the night that people imagine. (I should say that

I am speaking for myself, and for my father and my grandmother, who both died blind – blind, laughing, and brave, as I also hope to die. They inherited many things – blindness, for example – but one does not inherit courage. I know that they were brave.)

The blind live in a world that is inconvenient, an undefined world from which certain colors emerge: for me, yellow, blue (except that the blue may be green), and green (except that the green may be blue). White has disappeared, or is confused with grey. As for red, it has vanished completely. But I hope some day – I am following a treatment – to improve and to be able to see that great color, that color which shines in poetry, and which has so many beautiful names in many languages. Think of *scharlach* in German, *scarlet* in English, *escarlata* in Spanish, *écarlate* in French. Words that are worthy of that great color. In contrast, *amarillo*, yellow, sounds weak in Spanish; in English it seems more like yellow. I think that in Old Spanish it was *amariello*.

I live in that world of colors, and if I speak of my own modest blindness, I do so, first, because it is not the total blindness that people imagine, and second, because it deals with me. My case is not especially dramatic. What is dramatic are those who suddenly lose their sight. In my case, that slow nightfall, that slow loss of sight, began when I began to see. It has continued since 1899 without dramatic moments, a slow nightfall that has lasted more than three quarters of a century. In 1955, the pathetic moment came when I knew I had lost my sight, my reader's and writer's sight.

In my life I have received many unmerited honors, but

there is one that has made me happier than all the others: the directorship of the National Library. For reasons more political than literary, I was appointed by the Aramburu government.

I was named director of the library, and I returned to that building of which I had so many memories, on the Calle México in Monserrat, in the south of the city. I had never dreamed of the possibility of being director of the library. I had memories of another kind. I would go there with my father, at night. My father, a professor of psychology, would ask for some book by Bergson or William James, who were his favorite writers, or perhaps by Gustav Spiller. I, too timid to ask for a book, would look through some volume of the *Encyclopedia Britannica* or the German encyclopedias of Brockhaus or of Meyer. I would take a volume at random from the shelf and read. I remember one night when I was particularly rewarded, for I read three articles: on the Druids, the Druses, and Dryden – a gift of the letters *DR*. Other nights I was less fortunate.

I knew that Paul Groussac was in the building. I could have met him personally, but I was then quite shy; almost as shy as I am now. At the time, I believed that shyness was very important, but now I know that shyness is one of the evils one must try to overcome, that in reality to be shy doesn't matter – it is like so many other things to which one gives an exaggerated importance.

I received the nomination at the end of 1955. I was in charge, I was told, of a million books. Later I found out it was nine hundred thousand – a number that's more than enough. (And perhaps nine hundred thousand seems more than a million.)

Little by little I came to realize the strange irony of events. I had always imagined Paradise as a kind of library. Others think of a garden or of a palace. There I was, the center, in a way, of nine hundred thousand books in various languages, but I found I could barely make out the title pages and the spines. I wrote the 'Poem of the Gifts,' which begins:

> No one should read self-pity or reproach
> into this statement of the majesty
> of God; who with such splendid irony
> granted me books and blindness at one touch.

Those two gifts contradicted each other: the countless books and the night, the inability to read them.

I imagined the author of that poem to be Groussac, for Groussac was also the director of the library and also blind. Groussac was more courageous than I: he kept his silence. But I knew that there had certainly been moments when our lives had coincided, as we both had become blind and we both loved books. He honored literature with books far superior to mine. But we were both men of letters, and we both passed through the library of forbidden books – one might say, for our darkened eyes, of blank books, books without letters. I wrote of the irony of God, and in the end I asked myself which of us had written that poem of a plural I and a single shadow.

At the time I did not know that there had been another director of the library who was blind, José Mármol. Here appears the number three, which seals everything. Two is a mere coincidence; three, a confirmation. A confirmation of a ternary order, a divine or theological confirmation.

Mármol was director of the library when it was on the Calle Venezuela. These days it is usual to speak badly of Mármol, or not to mention him at all. But we must remember that when we speak of the time of Rosas, we do not think of the admirable book by Ramos Mejía, *Rosas and His Time*, but of the era as it is described in Mármol's wonderfully gossipy novel, *La Amalia*. To bequeath the image of an age or of a country is no small glory.

We have, then, three people who shared the same fate. And, for me, the joy of returning to the Monserrat section, in the Southside. For everyone in Buenos Aires, the Southside is, in a mysterious way, the secret center of the city. Not the other, somewhat ostentatious center we show to tourists – in those days there was not that bit of public relations called the Barrio de San Telmo. But the Southside has come to be the modest secret center of Buenos Aires.

When I think of Buenos Aires, I think of the Buenos Aires I knew as a child: the low houses, the patios, the porches, the cisterns with turtles in them, the grated windows. That Buenos Aires was all of Buenos Aires. Now only the southern section has been preserved. I felt that I had returned to the neighborhood of my elders.

There were the books, but I had to ask my friends the titles of them. I remembered a sentence from Rudolf Steiner, in his books on anthroposophy, which was the name he gave to his theosophy. He said that when something ends, we must think that something begins. His advice is salutary, but the execution is difficult, for we only know what we have lost, not what we will gain. We have a very precise image – an image at times shameless – of what we have lost, but we are ignorant of what may follow or replace it.

I made a decision. I said to myself: since I have lost the beloved world of appearances, I must create something else. At the time I was a professor of English at the university. What could I do to teach that almost infinite literature, that literature which exceeds the life of a man, and even generations of men? What could I do in four Argentine months of national holidays and strikes? I did what I could to teach the love of that literature, and I refrained as much as possible from dates and names.

Some female students came to see me. They had taken the exam and passed. (All students pass with me!) To the girls – there were nine or ten – I said: 'I have an idea. Now that you have passed and I have fulfilled my obligation as a professor, wouldn't it be interesting to embark on the study of a language or a literature we hardly know?' They asked which language and which literature. 'Well, naturally the English language and English literature. Let us begin to study them, now that we are free from the frivolity of the exams; let us begin at the beginning.'

I remembered that at home there were two books I could retrieve. I had placed them on the highest shelf, thinking I would never use them. They were Sweet's *Anglo-Saxon Reader* and *The Anglo-Saxon Chronicle*. Both had glossaries. And so we gathered one morning in the National Library.

I thought: I have lost the visible world, but now I am going to recover another, the world of my distant ancestors, those tribes of men who rowed across the stormy northern seas, from Germany, Denmark, and the Low Countries, who conquered England, and after whom we name England – since *Angle-land*, land of the Angles, had previously been called the land of the Britons, who were Celts.

It was a Saturday morning. We gathered in Groussac's office, and we began to read. There was a detail that pleased and mortified us, and at the same time filled us with a certain pride. It was the fact that the Saxons, like the Scandinavians, used two runic letters to signify the two sounds of *th*, as in 'thing' and 'the.' This conferred an air of mystery to the page.

We were encountering a language that seemed different from English but similar to German. What always happens, when one studies a language, happened. Each one of the words stood out as though it had been carved, as though it were a talisman. For that reason poems in a foreign language have a prestige they do not enjoy in their own language, for one hears, one sees, each one of the words individually. We think of the beauty, of the power, or simply of the strangeness of them.

We had good luck that morning. We discovered the sentence, 'Julius Caesar was the first Roman to discover England.' Finding ourselves with the Romans in a text of the North, we were moved. You must remember we knew nothing of the language; each word was a kind of talisman we unearthed. We found two words. And with those two words we became almost drunk. (It's true that I was an old man, and they were young women – likely stages for inebriation.) I thought: 'I am returning to the language my ancestors spoke fifty generations ago; I am returning to that language; I am reclaiming it. It is not the first time I speak it; when I had other names this was the language I spoke.' Those two words were the name of London, '*Lundenburh*,' and the name of Rome, which moved us even more, thinking of the light that had fallen on those northern islands, '*Romeburh*.' I think we left crying, 'Lundenburh, Romeburh . . .' in the streets.

So I began my study of Anglo-Saxon, which blindness brought me. And now I have a memory full of poetry that is elegiac, epic, Anglo-Saxon.

I had replaced the visible world with the aural world of the Anglo-Saxon language. Later I moved on to the richer world of Scandinavian literature: I went on to the *Eddas* and the sagas. I wrote *Ancient Germanic Literature* and many poems based on those themes, but most of all I enjoyed it. I am now preparing a book on Scandinavian literature.

I did not allow blindness to intimidate me. And besides, my publisher made me an excellent offer: he told me that if I produced thirty poems in a year, he would produce a book. Thirty poems means discipline, especially when one must dictate every line, but at the same time it allows for a sufficient freedom, as it is impossible that in one year there will not be thirty occasions for poetry. Blindness has not been for me a total misfortune; it should not be seen in a pathetic way. It should be seen as a way of life: one of the styles of living.

Being blind has its advantages. I owe to the darkness some gifts: the gift of Anglo-Saxon, my limited knowledge of Icelandic, the joy of so many lines of poetry, of so many poems, and of having written another book, entitled, with a certain falsehood, with a certain arrogance, *In Praise of Darkness*.

I would like to speak now of other cases, of illustrious cases. I will begin with that obvious example of the friendship of poetry and blindness, with the one who has been called the greatest of poets: Homer. (We know of another blind Greek poet, Tamiris, whose work has been lost. Tamiris was defeated in a battle with the Muses, who broke his lyre and took away his sight.)

Oscar Wilde had a curious hypothesis, one which I don't think is historically correct but which is intellectually agreeable. In general, writers try to make what they say seem profound; Wilde was a profound man who tried to seem frivolous. He wanted us to think of him as a conversationalist; he wanted us to consider him as Plato considered poetry, as 'that winged, fickle, sacred thing.' Well, that winged, fickle, sacred thing called Oscar Wilde said that Antiquity had deliberately represented Homer as blind.

We do not know if Homer existed. The fact that seven cities vie for his name is enough to make us doubt his historicity. Perhaps there was no single Homer; perhaps there were many Greeks whom we conceal under the name of Homer. The traditions are unanimous in showing us a blind poet, yet Homer's poetry is visual, often splendidly visual – as was, to a far lesser degree, that of Oscar Wilde.

Wilde realized that his own poetry was too visual, and he wanted to cure himself of that defect. He wanted to make poetry that was aural, musical – let us say like the poetry of Tennyson, or of Verlaine, whom he loved and admired so. Wilde said that the Greeks claimed that Homer was blind in order to emphasize that poetry must be aural, not visual. From that comes the *'de la musique avant toute chose'* of Verlaine and the symbolism contemporary to Wilde.

We may believe that Homer never existed, but that the Greeks imagined him as blind in order to insist on the fact that poetry is, above all, music; that poetry is, above all, the lyre; that the visual can or cannot exist in a poet. I know of great visual poets and great poets who are not visual – intellectual poets, mental ones – there's no need to mention names.

Let us go on to the example of Milton. Milton's blindness was voluntary. He knew from the beginning that he was going to be a great poet. This has occurred to other poets: Coleridge and De Quincey, before they wrote a single line, knew that their destiny was literary. I too, if I may mention myself, have always known that my destiny was, above all, a literary destiny – that bad things and some good things would happen to me, but that, in the long run, all of it would be converted into words. Particularly the bad things, since happiness does not need to be transformed: happiness is its own end.

Let us return to Milton. He destroyed his sight writing pamphlets in support of the execution of the king by Parliament. Milton said that he lost his sight voluntarily, defending freedom; he spoke of that noble task and never complained of being blind. He sacrificed his sight, and then he remembered his first desire, that of being a poet. They have discovered at Cambridge University a manuscript in which the young Milton proposes various subjects for a long poem.

'I might perhaps leave something so written to after-times, as they should not willingly let it die,' he declared. He listed some ten or fifteen subjects, not knowing that one of them would prove prophetic: the subject of Samson. He did not know that his fate would, in a way, be that of Samson; that Samson, who had prophesied Christ in the Old Testament, also prophesied Milton, and with greater accuracy. Once he knew himself to be perma-nently blind, he embarked on two historical works, *A Brief History of Muscovia* and *A History of England*, both of which remained unfinished, And then the long poem *Paradise Lost*. He sought a theme that would interest all men, not merely the English. That subject was Adam, our common father.

He spent a good part of his time alone, composing verses, and his memory had grown. He would hold forty or fifty hendecasyllables of blank verse in his memory and then dictate them to whomever came to visit. The whole poem was written in this way. He thought of the fate of Samson, so close to his own, for now Cromwell was dead and the hour of the Restoration had come. Mil-ton was persecuted and could have been condemned to death for having supported the execution of the king. But when they brought Charles II – son of Charles I, 'The Executed' – the list of those condemned to death, he put down his pen and said, not without nobility, 'There is something in my right hand which will not allow me to sign a sentence of death.' Milton was saved, and many others with him.

He then wrote *Samson Agonistes*. He wanted to create a Greek tragedy. The action takes place in a single day, Samson's last. Milton thought on the similarity of destinies, since he, like Samson, had been a strong man who was ultimately defeated. He was blind. And he wrote those verses which, according to Landor, he punctuated badly, but which in fact had to be 'Eyeless, in Gaza, at the mill, with the slaves' – as if the misfortunes were accumulating on Samson.

Milton has a sonnet in which he speaks of his blindness. There is a line one can tell was written by a blind man. When he has to describe the world, he says, 'In this dark world and wide.' It is precisely the world of the blind when they are alone, walking with hands outstretched, searching for props. Here we have an example – much more important than mine – of a man who overcomes blindness and does his work: *Paradise Lost, Paradise Regained, Samson Agonistes*, his best sonnets, part of *A History of England*, from the beginnings to the Norman Conquest. All of this was executed while he was blind; all of it had to be dictated to casual visitors.

The Boston aristocrat Prescott was helped by his wife. An accident, when he was a student at Harvard, had caused him to lose one eye and left him almost blind in the other. He decided that his life would be dedicated to literature. He studied, and learned, the literatures of England, France, Italy, and Spain. Imperial Spain offered him a world that was agreeable to his own rigid rejection of a democratic age. From an erudite he became a writer, and he dictated to his wife the histories of the conquest of Mexico and Peru, of the reign of the Catholic Kings and of Phillip II. It was a happy labor, almost impeccable, which took more than twenty years.

There are two examples that are closer to us. One I have already mentioned, Paul Groussac, who has been unjustly forgotten. People see him now as a French interloper in Argentina. It is said that his historical work has become dated, that today one makes use of greater documentation. But they forget that Groussac, like every writer, left two works: first, his subject, and second, the manner of its execution. Groussac revitalized Spanish prose. Alfonso Reyes, the greatest prose writer in Spanish in any era, once told me, 'Groussac taught me how Spanish should be written.' Groussac overcame his blindness and left some of the best pages in prose that have been written in our country. It will always please me to remember this.

Let us recall another example, one more famous than Groussac. In James Joyce we are also given a twofold work. We have those two vast and – why not say it? – unreadable novels, *Ulysses* and *Finnegans Wake*. But that is only half of his work (which also includes beautiful poems and the admirable *Portrait of an Artist as a Young Man*). The other half, and perhaps the most redeeming aspect (as they now say) is the fact that he took on the almost infinite English language. That language – which is statistically larger than all the others and offers so many possibilities for the writer, particularly in its concrete verbs – was not enough for him. Joyce, an Irishman, recalled that Dublin had been founded by Danish Vikings. He studied Norwegian – he wrote a letter to Ibsen in Norwegian – and then he studied Greek, Latin. . . . He knew all the languages, and he wrote in a language invented by himself, difficult to understand but marked by a strange music. Joyce brought a new music to English. And he said, valorously (and mendaciously) that 'of all the things that have happened to me, I think the least important was having been blind.' Part of his vast work was executed in darkness: polishing the sentences in his memory, working at times for a whole day on a single phrase, and then writing it and correcting it. All in the midst of blindness or periods of blindness. In comparison, the impotence of Boileau, Swift, Kant, Ruskin, and George Moore was a melancholic instrument for the successful execution of their work; one might say the same of perversion, whose beneficiaries today have ensured that no one will ignore their names. Democritus of Abdera tore his eyes out in a garden so that the spectacle of reality would not distract him; Origen castrated himself.

I have enumerated enough examples. Some are so illustrious that I am ashamed to have spoken of my own personal case – except for the fact that people always hope for confessions, and I have no reason to deny them mine. But, of course, it seems absurd to place my name next to those I have recalled.

I have said that blindness is a way of life, a way of life that is not entirely unfortunate. Let us recall those lines of the greatest Spanish poet, Fray Luis de León:

> *Vivir quiero conmigo,*
> *gozar quiero del bien que debo al cielo,*
> *a solas sin testigo,*
> *libre de amor, de celo,*
> *de odio, de esperanza, de recelo.*

[I want to live with myself, / I want to enjoy the good
that I owe to heaven, / alone, without witnesses, / free of
love, of jealousy, / of hate, of hope, of fear.]

Edgar Allan Poe knew this stanza by heart.

For me, to live without hate is easy, for I have never felt
hate. To live without love I think is impossible, happily
impossible for each one of us. But the first part – 'I want
to live with myself, / I want to enjoy the good that I owe to
heaven' – if we accept that in the good of heaven there
can also be darkness, then who lives more with themselves? Who can explore themselves more? Who can
know more of themselves? According to the Socratic
phrase, who can know himself more than the blind man?

A writer lives. The task of being a poet is not completed
at a fixed schedule. No one is a poet from eight to twelve
and from two to six. Whoever is a poet is always one, and
continually assaulted by poetry. I suppose a painter feels
that colors and shapes are besieging him. Or a musician
feels that the strange world of sounds – the strangest world
of art – is always seeking him out, that there are melodies
and dissonances looking for him. For the task of an artist,
blindness is not a total misfortune. It may be an instrument.
Fray Luis de León dedicated one of his most beautiful
odes to Francisco Salinas, a blind musician.

A writer, or any man, must believe that whatever happens to him is an instrument; everything has been given
for an end. This is even stronger in the case of the artist.
Everything that happens, including humiliations, embar-
rassments, misfortunes, all has been given like clay, like
material for one's art. One must accept it. For this reason

I speak in a poem of the ancient food of heroes: humiliation, unhappiness, discord. Those things are given to us to transform, so that we may make from the miserable circumstances of our lives things that are eternal, or aspire to be so.

If a blind man thinks this way, he is saved. Blindness is a gift. I have exhausted you with the gifts it has given me. It gave me Anglo-Saxon, it gave me some Scandinavian, it gave me a knowledge of a medieval literature I didn't know, it gave me the writing of various books, good or bad, but which justified the moment in which they were written. Moreover, blindness has made me feel surrounded by the kindness of others. People always feel good will toward the blind.

I want to end with a line of Goethe: *'Alles Nahe werde fern,'* everything near becomes far. Goethe was referring to the evening twilight. Everything near becomes far. It is true. At nightfall, the things closest to us seem to move away from our eyes. So the visible world has moved away from my eyes, perhaps forever.

Goethe could be referring not only to twilight but to life. All things go off, leaving us. Old age is probably the supreme solitude – except that the supreme solitude is death. And 'everything near becomes far' also refers to the slow process of blindness, of which I hoped to show, speaking tonight, that it is not a complete misfortune. It is one more instrument among the many – all of them so strange – that fate or chance provide.

[1977]

1. Seneca *On the Shortness of Life*
2. Marcus Aurelius *Meditations*
3. St Augustine *Confessions of a Sinner*
4. Thomas à Kempis *The Inner Life*
5. Niccolò Machiavelli *The Prince*
6. Michel de Montaigne *On Friendship*
7. Jonathan Swift *A Tale of a Tub*
8. Jean-Jacques Rousseau *The Social Contract*
9. Edward Gibbon *The Christians and the Fall of Rome*
10. Thomas Paine *Common Sense*
11. Mary Wollstonecraft *A Vindication of the Rights of Woman*
12. William Hazlitt *On the Pleasure of Hating*
13. Karl Marx & Friedrich Engels *The Communist Manifesto*
14. Arthur Schopenhauer *On the Suffering of the World*
15. John Ruskin *On Art and Life*
16. Charles Darwin *On Natural Selection*
17. Friedrich Nietzsche *Why I am So Wise*
18. Virginia Woolf *A Room of One's Own*
19. Sigmund Freud *Civilization and Its Discontents*
20. George Orwell *Why I Write*

21. Confucius *The First Ten Books*
22. Sun-tzu *The Art of War*
23. Plato *The Symposium*
24. Lucretius *Sensation and Sex*
25. Cicero *An Attack on an Enemy of Freedom*
26. *The Revelation of St John the Divine* and *The Book of Job*
27. Marco Polo *Travels in the Land of Kubilai Khan*
28. Christine de Pizan *The City of Ladies*
29. Baldesar Castiglione *How to Achieve True Greatness*
30. Francis Bacon *Of Empire*
31. Thomas Hobbes *Of Man*
32. Sir Thomas Browne *Urne-Burial*
33. Voltaire *Miracles and Idolatry*
34. David Hume *On Suicide*
35. Carl von Clausewitz *On the Nature of War*
36. Søren Kierkegaard *Fear and Trembling*
37. Henry David Thoreau *Where I Lived, and What I Lived For*
38. Thorstein Veblen *Conspicuous Consumption*
39. Albert Camus *The Myth of Sisyphus*
40. Hannah Arendt *Eichmann and the Holocaust*

41. Plutarch *In Consolation to his Wife*
42. Robert Burton *Some Anatomies of Melancholy*
43. Blaise Pascal *Human Happiness*
44. Adam Smith *The Invisible Hand*
45. Edmund Burke *The Evils of Revolution*
46. Ralph Waldo Emerson *Nature*
47. Søren Kierkegaard *The Sickness unto Death*
48. John Ruskin *The Lamp of Memory*
49. Friedrich Nietzsche *Man Alone with Himself*
50. Leo Tolstoy *A Confession*
51. William Morris *Useful Work v. Useless Toil*
52. Frederick Jackson Turner *The Significance of the Frontier in American History*
53. Marcel Proust *Days of Reading*
54. Leon Trotsky *An Appeal to the Toiling, Oppressed and Exhausted Peoples of Europe*
55. Sigmund Freud *The Future of an Illusion*
56. Walter Benjamin *The Work of Art in the Age of Mechanical Reproduction*
57. George Orwell *Books v. Cigarettes*
58. Albert Camus *The Fastidious Assassins*
59. Frantz Fanon *Concerning Violence*
60. Michel Foucault *The Spectacle of the Scaffold*

61. Lao Tzu *Tao Te Ching*
62. *Writings from the Zen Masters*
63. Thomas More *Utopia*
64. Michel de Montaigne *On Solitude*
65. William Shakespeare *On Power*
66. John Locke *Of the Abuse of Words*
67. Samuel Johnson *Consolation in the Face of Death*
68. Immanuel Kant *An Answer to the Question: 'What is Enlightenment?'*
69. Joseph de Maistre *The Executioner*
70. Thomas De Quincey *Confessions of an English Opium Eater*
71. Arthur Schopenhauer *The Horrors and Absurdities of Religion*
72. Abraham Lincoln *The Gettysburg Address*
73. Karl Marx *Revolution and War*
74. Fyodor Dostoyevsky *The Grand Inquisitor*
75. William James *On a Certain Blindness in Human Beings*
76. Robert Louis Stevenson *An Apology for Idlers*
77. W. E. B. Du Bois *Of the Dawn of Freedom*
78. Virginia Woolf *Thoughts on Peace in an Air Raid*
79. George Orwell *Decline of the English Murder*
80. John Berger *Why Look at Animals?*

81. Chuang Tzu *The Tao of Nature*
82. Epictetus *Of Human Freedom*
83. Niccolò Machiavelli *On Conspiracies*
84. René Descartes *Meditations*
85. Giacomo Leopardi *Dialogue Between Fashion and Death*
86. John Stuart Mill *On Liberty*
87. Charles Darwin *Hosts of Living Forms*
88. Charles Dickens *Night Walks*
89. Charles Mackay *Some Extraordinary Popular Delusions*
90. Jacob Burckhardt *The State as a Work of Art*
91. George Eliot *Silly Novels by Lady Novelists*
92. Charles Baudelaire *The Painter of Modern Life*
93. Sigmund Freud *The 'Wolfman'*
94. Theodor Herzl *The Jewish State*
95. Rabindranath Tagore *Nationalism*
96. Vladimir Ilyich Lenin *Imperialism*
97. Winston Churchill *We Will All Go Down Fighting to the End*
98. Jorge Luis Borges *The Perpetual Race of Achilles and the Tortoise*
99. George Orwell *Some Thoughts on the Common Toad*
100. Chinua Achebe *An Image of Africa*

THE STORY OF PENGUIN CLASSICS

Before 1946 ... 'Classics' are mainly the domain of academics and students; readable editions for everyone else are almost unheard of. This all changes when a little-known classicist, E. V. Rieu, presents Penguin founder Allen Lane with the translation of Homer's *Odyssey* that he has been working on in his spare time.

1946 Penguin Classics debuts with *The Odyssey*, which promptly sells three million copies. Suddenly, classics are no longer for the privileged few.

1950s Rieu, now series editor, turns to professional writers for the best modern, readable translations, including Dorothy L. Sayers's *Inferno* and Robert Graves's unexpurgated *Twelve Caesars*.

1960s The Classics are given the distinctive black covers that have remained a constant throughout the life of the series. Rieu retires in 1964, hailing the Penguin Classics list as 'the greatest educative force of the twentieth century.'

1970s A new generation of translators swells the Penguin Classics ranks, introducing readers of English to classics of world literature from more than twenty languages. The list grows to encompass more history, philosophy, science, religion and politics.

1980s The Penguin American Library launches with titles such as *Uncle Tom's Cabin*, and joins forces with Penguin Classics to provide the most comprehensive library of world literature available from any paperback publisher.

1990s The launch of Penguin Audiobooks brings the classics to a listening audience for the first time, and in 1999 the worldwide launch of the Penguin Classics website extends their reach to the global online community.

The 21st Century Penguin Classics are completely redesigned for the first time in nearly twenty years. This world-famous series now consists of more than 1300 titles, making the widest range of the best books ever written available to millions – and constantly redefining what makes a 'classic'.

The Odyssey continues ...

The best books ever written

PENGUIN  CLASSICS

SINCE 1946

Find out more at www.penguinclassics.com